"The good news is as Jewish as Jesus is, and Jennifer Rosner's warm, insightful work invites readers to take a fresh look at what this means for their faith. Her exploration of subjects that often have been issues of confusion when considering the Jewish foundations of faith in Jesus, such as ritual purity, holy days, and the apostle Paul's writing, are grounded in both careful scholarship and deeply rooted faith in Messiah Jesus. As a Jewish believer, I am grateful for *Finding Messiah* and the conversations I know it will spark in the church."

Michelle Van Loon, author of *Moments & Days: How Our Holy Celebrations Shape Our Faith*

"Look no further. This is the most enjoyable introduction to Jesus and Judaism you will ever find. It is Professor Rosner's personal story of religious exploration through her fascinating life of study and love in California and Israel. It is precise in its account of scholarly debates but also perfectly accessible to nonscholars. Recommended to all."

Gerald McDermott, Beeson Divinity School (retired), author of *Israel Matters*

"Formative years in the Vineyard movement taught Jennifer Rosner to bear testimonial witness to Jesus in the power of the Spirit. This book testifies of her loves—of Yonah, her husband (theologians fall in love too!), of Jesus the Messiah (here a Jewish person is grasped by his love!), and of historic and contemporary Jewish faith and practice (how one can fall in love with the tradition one was raised in all over again!). Spoiler alert: Christians and Jews, including theologians from both faiths, who read this book will need to be prepared to be challenged by Rosner's powerful theological narrative that cuts right to the core of the biblical message!"

Amos Yong, Fuller Seminary

"This is a book I didn't know I was waiting for. As a Jewish follower of Jesus, Jen has affirmed much of my own experience and bore witness to something meaningful that God is doing. She has challenged me to reconsider things I thought settled and has taught me other things I did not know. She has done all of this in a volume that is brilliantly and cleverly arranged, using the pleasant sharing of her own story as a guide. It is another book that will serve as a marker for the larger conversation about reckoning the Jewishness of the Christian faith and Jewish identity in the world today."

Marty Solomon, creator and executive producer of the BEMA Podcast and president of Impact Campus Ministries

"So much theology is written as though nothing much is at stake. But to read Jen Rosner, the stakes could not be higher: draining Christianity of the poison of anti-Judaism and showing her fellow Jews that she can be a loyal daughter of Sarah and follower of Jesus. I'm not sure which is the taller task! But I do know this: she has written a beautiful and brave and learned book, and you should read it."

Jason Byassee, Vancouver School of Theology, author of *Surprised by Jesus Again*

"How odd that one of the Bible's main themes—God's love for the Jewish people—is so often missing from textbooks on Christian theology. In this book, Jen Rosner interweaves autobiography, interpretation of Scripture, liturgics, doctrinal analysis, and historical investigation to fill in the gap. The result is an illuminating study that is likely to challenge and change the way you understand the gospel of Jesus Christ."

R. Kendall Soulen, professor of systematic theology at Candler School of Theology, Emory University

"In *Finding Messiah*, Jennifer M. Rosner deftly weaves together her fascinating story of becoming a Jewish follower of Jesus with her adept theological investigation into the questions and implications surrounding Messianic Christianity. Rosner's attempt to bridge the ancient rift between Jewish identity and Christian faith is timely and important. I thoroughly enjoyed this book."

Brian Zahnd, author of *When Everything's on Fire*

"Jen Rosner interweaves her fascinating journey as a Messianic Jew navigating the tensions between Judaism and Christianity with an informative discussion of the Judaism of the earliest believers in Jesus. I heartily recommend her work here. Christians everywhere need to learn more about the Jewishness of the New Testament and the necessity of understanding of Jesus and Paul within their original Hebraic context."

Lois Tverberg, author of *Reading the Bible with Rabbi Jesus*

FINDING MESSIAH

A Journey
into the
Jewishness
of the
Gospel

∽·∽·∽

Jennifer M. Rosner
Foreword by Richard J. Mouw

An imprint of InterVarsity Press
Downers Grove, Illinois

InterVarsity Press
P.O. Box 1400, Downers Grove, IL 60515-1426
ivpress.com
email@ivpress.com

InterVarsity Press® is the book-publishing division of InterVarsity Christian Fellowship/USA®,
a movement of students and faculty active on campus at hundreds of universities, colleges, and schools
of nursing in the United States of America, and a member movement of the International Fellowship
of Evangelical Students. For information about local and regional activities, visit intervarsity.org.

All Scripture quotations, unless otherwise indicated, are taken from The Holy Bible, New International
Version®, NIV®. Copyright © 1973, 1978, 1984, 2011 by Biblica, Inc.™ Used by permission of Zondervan.
All rights reserved worldwide. www.zondervan.com. The "NIV" and "New International Version" are
trademarks registered in the United States Patent and Trademark Office by Biblica, Inc.™

While any stories in this book are true, some names and identifying information may have been changed
to protect the privacy of individuals.

The publisher cannot verify the accuracy or functionality of website URLs used in this book beyond
the date of publication.

Cover design and image composite: David Fassett
Interior design: Daniel van Loon
Image: tallit image © Erin Ebright

ISBN 978-1-5140-0324-4 (print)
ISBN 978-1-5140-0325-1 (digital)

Printed in the United States of America ♾

InterVarsity Press is committed to ecological stewardship and to the conservation of natural resources
in all our operations. This book was printed using sustainably sourced paper.

Library of Congress Cataloging-in-Publication Data

Names: Rosner, Jennifer M., author.
Title: Finding messiah : a journey into the Jewishness of the Gospel /
    Jennifer M. Rosner.
Description: Downers Grove : InterVarsity Press, [2022] | Includes
    bibliographical references.
Identifiers: LCCN 2021061340 (print) | LCCN 2021061341 (ebook) | ISBN
    9781514003244 (paperback) | ISBN 9781514003251 (ebook)
Subjects: LCSH: Messianic Judaism. | Christianity—Origin. |
    Judaism—Relations—Christianity. | Christianity and other
    religions—Judaism. | Rosner, Jennifer M.
Classification: LCC BR158 .R67 2022 (print) | LCC BR158 (ebook) | DDC
    289.9—dc23/eng/20220111
LC record available at https://lccn.loc.gov/2021061340
LC ebook record available at https://lccn.loc.gov/2021061341

P   25   24   23   22   21   20   19   18   17   16   15   14   13   12   11   10   9   8   7   6   5   4   3   2   1

Y   41   40   39   38   37   36   35   34   33   32   31   30   29   28   27   26   25   24   23   22

This book is dedicated to my parents,

whose love and support for us truly know no bounds.

MOM,

you are not afraid to ask the hard questions of faith
and you never fail to fill my children with wonder.

DAD,

you daily model humility and integrity, and
you always make time for one more game of Candyland with the kids.

To both of you, we are so very grateful.

CONTENTS

FOREWORD

Richard J. Mouw

As I read Jen Rosner tell her unfolding story about what her Jewishness means for her faith in Christ, I was prompted to reflect on my own life and journey. I found myself thinking back to key moments and relationships that have shaped my understanding of the important topics she explores.

The first relationship I could remember occurred when, as a thirteen-year-old Boy Scout, I formed a special friendship with Bobby Silverstein, the only Jewish kid in the troop. Every one of our Scout meetings began with all of us citing the "Scout Law" together. For most of the others that seemed to be a perfunctory exercise, but Bobby and I liked to talk about what the list of virtues we recited meant for our young lives. Bobby once told me that he did not know why God would require that a Jewish Boy Scout be "cheerful," given all the horrible things the Nazis had done to Jewish people. I agreed with him, and I decided that God was asking me to be distressed by that also.

Other friendships I had experienced along the way kept coming up as I read Jen's book. But the big theological topic that she has forced me to think about more deeply than I have wanted to is "replacement theology." I had once endorsed this perspective in something I had written, where I observed that the apostle Peter refers to the New Testament church as a "chosen race" and "holy nation," thus taking images that had once applied to the ancient Israelites and now reassigning them to the community of Gentile and Jewish followers of Jesus. This meant, I had argued, that we Christians are now, as "the new Israel," the beneficiaries of the covenantal blessings that had once been promised to "the old Israel."

After making that case in the 1970s, I began to question those replacement ideas. Much of the change in my thinking was simply finding myself learning from Jewish sources: Chaim Potok's novels, Martin Buber's ethical writings, Abraham Joshua Heschel's rich expositions of the Bible's prophetic literature, and illuminating thoughts over kosher lunches with rabbi friends. Gradually I began to think of God's covenant with Gentile Christians, not as replacing the older covenant with Israel, but that the church has been "grafted onto" God's ancient covenant people.

That was an important shift for me, but I did leave a lot of things hanging. Some of the key issues I chose to ignore were being raised by Messianic Jews, but I found them too complex to wrestle with. What about Jewish followers of Yeshua who observe the Torah's commandments to the Jewish people, understanding them to be enduring and not replaced by new covenant particulars? How should the evangelical community relate to Messianic Jews? How did the early Christians understand their practice of continuing to worship in synagogues? And, what in the world was Paul getting at in Romans 9?

I had been content to leave all of that hanging, but as I read Jen's book, I realized that she was not going to let me off the hook on any of it. The fact that her wrestling with these issues has meant for her complex and at times deeply painful struggles forced me to do some serious wrestling of my own.

I met Jen for the first time when she began her doctoral studies at Fuller Seminary. She told me that as a Jewish follower of Jesus she was interested in using Karl Barth's theology to explore issues in Judaism. When I casually asked her if she saw herself as a Messianic Jew, she paused a bit before responding that this was becoming a big question in her life.

Further along in her time at Fuller, I became aware of the difficulties she faced—and agonized over—as a student participant in interfaith events for seminary students, where Jewish-Christian relations were an intentional focus. But mainly I watched her from a distance, reading some of her dissertation-related research papers where she critically engaged the views of Jewish and Christian scholars.

Now, following her journey in these pages, I see how engaging these theological issues has affected her, not only as a gifted doctoral student but also as a teacher, a wife, a mother—and as a member of the Jesus-following Jewish community, which has regularly been seriously misunderstood, theologically and spiritually, by both Christians and Jews.

So, yes, Jen Rosner has forced me to face issues that I have long been willing to ignore, and I will now continue to face. I am confident that her wonderful book will motivate others to make the journey also. Jen still has questions that she is pursuing, so it has to be a continuing journey for all of us. For now, though, I can express deep gratitude that she has prodded me to take some new steps along the path!

INTRODUCTION

On Being Monstrous

*It is monstrous to talk of Jesus Christ
and to practice Judaism.*

<small>Ignatius of Antioch</small>

St. John's Episcopal Church is a brown stone building that stands unassumingly on the corner of Orange Street and Humphrey Street in New Haven, Connecticut, a six-block walk from my apartment. I had tried several different churches since moving to New Haven the previous year, none of which felt like a particularly good fit. I was intimidated about attending St. John's, as a number of my professors from Yale Divinity School worshiped there, and it felt awkward to "casually" chat with them over coffee cake after the service, all the while secretly wondering if they had read my research paper yet and if I had accurately characterized the theology of Karl Rahner.

I attended St. John's for the first time in the winter of 2004. This was my first experience with Episcopal tradition, and I spent the entire time just trying to keep up with what was going on. Stand up, sit down, red book, blue book, kneel, recite congregational responses. I caught nothing of the flow or careful ordering of the service, and I was baffled at how anyone could find this kind of worship meaningful.

Just a few years prior, I had become a follower of Jesus in a Vineyard church (causing, I might add, quite a stir in my Jewish family). I loved the casual, Spirit-led worship of the Vineyard, and high church liturgy was entirely lost on me.

Thankfully, I went back. Something about the time-worn prayers (and pews) beckoned me to return. Instinctually, I knew there was more to be uncovered than what was obvious on first blush.

Slowly, despite my liturgical clumsiness and enduring intimidation, St. John's made itself my church home for the next year and a half. The rhythm of the service became deeply meaningful for me, and the rituals we rehearsed each week—the confession of the Nicene Creed, the Great Thanksgiving, processing to the front and kneeling to receive the Eucharist—nourished my soul in a season where all that seemed to matter during the week was my brain.

As I look back, it makes even more sense why I ended up at St. John's during my time at Yale. It wasn't just because the lively fellowship hall was where my professors gradually became human beings with spouses and mortgages and sticky-fingered children who on occasion misbehaved. It wasn't just because it afforded me the ability to walk to church, a practice I had come to cherish.

I now see that in a strange way, liturgical worship (like what I came to love at St. John's) is the closest thing Christianity has to traditional Judaism. The printed prayers on the pages of bound books, the embodied movements of standing, sitting, and kneeling, the sacralized consumption of certain foods—this was all Judaism stripped of its name and repackaged in Christian garb.

Even my seemingly trivial desire to walk to church, I now realize, was an inherently Jewish impulse. For religious Jews, there is no driving across town to be a part of *that* worshiping community, because there is no driving on Shabbat. You worship close to home, at your local synagogue, with your neighbors and friends.

Of course, none of these connections are apparent to the untrained eye. The Jesus who was preached at St. John's rarely looked like a Jewish rabbi who would not have eaten many of the foods served at the church's Christmas potluck. In many ways, St. John's—like most other churches in the world—was very much the fulfillment of Ignatius's prophetic invective: "It is monstrous to talk of Jesus Christ and to practice Judaism." Practicing any kind of Judaism amid the thoroughly high church atmosphere of St. John's might not have quite reached the level of "monstrous," but it would have certainly seemed quite foreign and out of place.

History, however, reveals that this was not always the case, and the development as such was far from inevitable. Jesus was indeed a Jewish rabbi whose life was patterned around the Jewish calendar, not the Christian calendar. As well as being the Savior of the world, he celebrated Passover with his disciples, taught in synagogues, and wore *tzitzit* (the traditional fringed garment commanded in Numbers 15).

So, what happened? How did the church forget that the incarnate God was an observant Jew? How has Jesus' identity as Israel's long promised Messiah become such a fuzzy concept in Christian thought? Why have the practices that inscribed Jesus' life—things like the Sabbath, pilgrimage to Jerusalem, and engaging the forces of ritual impurity—become sheer oddities in Christian faith and devotion? How have issues that deeply preoccupied the early church (things like table fellowship between

Jews and Gentiles, the role of circumcision, and faithfulness to the commandments given in the Torah) become tabooed tangents in modern Christian life? How have the embodied practices of a living faith—which stand at the heart of Jewish life—become largely lost in contemporary Christian discipleship? How, in short, has Christianity wandered so very far away from Judaism?

This book is an attempt to dive into this set of issues and questions. My goal is to retrace the history that ultimately declared Judaism and Christianity to be two separate (and largely incompatible) religious traditions and to challenge the conclusions that are often drawn as a result of that history.

I am primarily writing to Christians, perhaps especially Christian leaders, who find themselves deeply invested in their own church traditions but who feel intrigued by what a deeper knowledge of Judaism might add to Christian faith. In the end, my hope is that this book will enrich your spiritual practices and add to your understanding of the thoroughly Jewish foundation that Christianity has in many ways moved away from.

As we begin to ponder the utter separateness between Judaism and Christianity, Ignatius's words give us a clue to this puzzle whose pieces are hidden in the folds of history. As Messianic Jewish theologian Mark Kinzer points out, Ignatius's efforts to draw a thick black line between Christians and Jews are proof that such a line did not yet exist. Rather, Ignatius was among those who successfully sought to create a new religion called Christianity that would eventually unhitch itself from what they perceived to be the tired and heavy yoke of Judaism.[1]

But for some of us, like myself, this parting of the ways is a great tragedy. It is the first and deepest church split. While one painful ramification of this split is that it leaves no room for Jewish followers of Jesus to live as Jews, an even greater problem is that it mars the true identity of the church itself. As Paul reminds us in Romans 11, Gentile (i.e., non-Jewish) followers of Jesus are "grafted in" to God's covenantal relationship with Israel. The church is joined together with God's existing covenant people, not a law-free, grace-based replacement of that people.

Fast forward almost twenty years from my first visit to St. John's. I now call myself a Messianic Jew, I am married to another Messianic Jew, and we have two young children. The rhythm of our lives is decidedly Jewish. We observe the weekly Jewish *Shabbat* (Sabbath) that begins on Friday night and ends on Saturday night. I make *challah*, the traditional Jewish braided bread, which we eat after reciting *hamotzi*, the Jewish blessing over bread. In the darkest nights of winter, our home is illumined by the bright light of Hanukkah candles. Our stomachs growl and groan during the annual fast of Yom Kippur (The Day of Atonement), and our home is cleared of all *chametz* (leaven) before Passover comes.

However, we also believe that Jesus (we call him by his Hebrew name, Yeshua) was God incarnate and took away the sins of the world. We read our children stories from the Gospels, and we recite with them both the Lord's Prayer and Judaism's central declaration of God's oneness, the Shema.

Like other Jewish followers of Jesus, our lives are spent trying to forge a way between two religions that have spent roughly sixteen centuries defining themselves in opposition to one another. Bending back the deeply entrenched patterns of history is not easy work. It's a lonely path, and we are often misunderstood.

But for us, there's no other authentic way to live out our faith. As my friend Ben Ehrenfeld once put it, "Asking me to choose between Jesus and Judaism is like asking me to choose between my heart and my lungs." For us, there is only the in-between path, the third way that history has erased.

In reinventing this path, in forging it once again, I am convinced that we will rediscover our Lord and Messiah. In the pages that follow, I invite you to join me on this journey.

1

THE PARTING OF THE WAYS

The parting of the ways was more between mainstream
Christianity and Jewish Christianity than simply between
Christianity as a single whole and rabbinic Judaism.

JAMES DUNN

W e made it!" my sister-in-law Leila exclaimed as we pulled
into the parking garage of my new apartment complex in
Pasadena, marking the end of our week-long cross-country
girls' trip.

I shut off the car. "Yep, I guess this is my new home." I tried to
keep my voice light, but in truth I was feeling overwhelmed. Soon,
my three constant companions of the past seven days (Leila and
two close friends) would return to their familiar lives in Northern
California, while I began the exciting but undeniably daunting
process of starting over again in a new city.

Having finished my MDiv at Yale, I was now back in California
to begin working on my PhD at Fuller Theological Seminary. My
years at Yale had gifted me with a profound love for Christian

theology (especially that of Karl Barth), yet toward the end of my time there, a startling realization had begun to crystallize: my deep and abiding Christian faith had almost completely eclipsed the Judaism of my heritage and upbringing. I felt like I had lost an anchoring piece of my identity, and I didn't know what it looked like to get it back.

I was raised in a Jewish home in Northern California, where my parents had moved one week after getting married. They were both raised in Los Angeles, my mom in the Reform Jewish movement and my dad in the Conservative Jewish movement.[1] As I grew up, my mom worked hard to preserve Jewish traditions and practices in our home while my dad dedicated himself to instilling in my brother and me a solid and grounding faith in God.

The spirituality of my parents didn't always line up, as my dad was also influenced by the New Age movement and held a certain suspicion of organized religion. My mom was agnostic until well into their marriage, but the rhythms of Jewish life were an anchoring part of her identity. We never got plugged into the local Jewish community, which both of my parents found to be too liberal.

My sense of Jewish identity was sturdy, even if I wasn't always sure what that meant or implied. My undergraduate years at Cal Poly, a large public state university, became a time of deep searching, and it "just so happened" that most of my friends in college were Christians. I found myself increasingly considering the claims of Christianity while being in part unable to connect with the more secular Hillel (Jewish student group) on my college campus.

I had chosen Cal Poly largely because that's where my brother was studying, and I look back fondly at our weekly sibling dinner nights where we would share about our lives and friendships, our faith and fears. My last year in college, through a series of powerful events, the claims of Jesus became undeniable and I yielded my life to following him. Remarkably, sparked by a short-lived dating relationship with my Christian roommate, my brother also came to faith in Jesus in college. At the time, I had no idea what belief in Jesus meant for my Jewishness, so I simply buried it.

I became deeply involved with a Vineyard church plant and seldom spoke of my Jewish upbringing and identity. My bachelor's degree is in political science, and I had planned to go to law school like many of the students in my department. However, upon stumbling into faith in Jesus, I was immediately awakened to a profound fascination with theology that led me to divinity school instead. During my years at Yale I had felt like a kid in a candy shop, reveling in church history, systematic theology, and biblical languages.

But now, I was faced with a new dilemma. As my long-ignored Jewish identity started clamoring for attention, I began to wonder how on earth I could be both Jewish and Christian. These tensions would rise to the fore during my doctoral program.

Upon arriving at Fuller, I once again commenced the tiresome process of trying to find a new church home. For a year, I schlepped all the way across Los Angeles to attend Bel Air Presbyterian Church. After that, I spent six months attending a little Evangelical Free church whose white building stood on a shady residential street that was walking distance from my apartment. And, just like in New Haven, I once again ended up at an Episcopal church.

This particular Episcopal church—St. James' in South Pasadena— had as its associate priest a Palestinian Christian named Sari. I spent two years attending St. James', and I will forever be grateful for the friendship that I developed with Sari and his family, which became the font of much deeply enriching conversation, co-teaching, and building our own small but strong bridge across the chasm that often divides Jews and Arabs.

I probably would have stayed at St. James' a lot longer had a quiet yet persistent subplot not begun developing in my life. My first year at Fuller, I nonchalantly revealed to my doctoral adviser, Howard Loewen, that I was Jewish. At Yale, my experience of theology was that it didn't much matter who was doing the theologizing, it just mattered that it was solid and innovative. But the particulars of my spiritual identity were about to take on new meaning.

"You're Jewish?" marveled Howard following my reveal, eyes slightly wide. "That *matters*. You must meet my friend Mark Kinzer." What I would discover throughout the remainder of my doctoral program was that Mark Kinzer is one of the leading voices in the contemporary Messianic Jewish movement (which is largely composed of followers of Jesus committed to preserving Jewish identity), and that who I am matters profoundly in the way that I approach Christian theology.

About a month later, I sat at a corner table in a local coffee shop across from Mark Kinzer, who was in town for a conference and who assured me that there were lots of other people "like us" out there. One such person was Stuart Dauermann, who at the time led a Messianic Jewish congregation (something I had never even heard of) in Beverly Hills.

A number of things happened over the next several years. I began attending Stuart's congregation and, even amid the awkwardness and unfamiliarity of another new faith community, something about the Jewish rhythms touched deep inside my soul. It became abundantly clear to me why no church or denomination had ever quite felt like "home" to me. Messianic Jewish congregations can be complex places, as any in-between existence is. But in a flash, I knew that this in-between life lived alongside other Jewish followers of Jesus was my spiritual home.

The second thing that happened was that my own inner struggle to find my way as a newly self-identified Messianic Jew spilled over into my academic work. I ended up writing my doctoral dissertation on the ways in which the mutually exclusive categories bequeathed to us by the parting of the ways are being called into question in certain circles in our own day.[2] And just like that, I was hooked. I knew it would be my life's passion to break open the common misperceptions about Judaism and Christianity and the gap between them.

꽃·꽃·꽃

While most people are aware that Jesus was Jewish (as were the apostles), the significance and implications of this identity marker are often left unexplored. These founders of Christianity worshiped in the Jerusalem temple, lived in booths during the holiday of Sukkot, and upheld the statutes of the Torah. They were wholly committed to the Jewish faith, and this context influenced how the apostles understood who Jesus was and what following him entailed. The eventual parting of the ways between Judaism and Christianity was a complex process whereby each developing religious community sought to distance itself from the other, the result being two entirely separate religions. I don't think Jesus' first followers saw this coming.

The New Testament seeks to envision and build a community where both Jews and Gentiles follow Jesus, the Jewish Messiah, side by side. As we see in Acts 10, Peter is astonished that the Spirit comes on Gentiles just as the Spirit came upon Jews in Acts 2. "I now realize how true it is that God does not show favoritism but accepts from every nation the one who fears him and does what is right," Peter marvels in Acts 10:34-35. Apparently, even Jesus' inner circle did not realize the full impact of his coming up until this point.

The rest of the book of Acts describes the process of how this early Jesus-following community sought to forge the way forward. Do Gentile followers of Jesus need to take on Jewish practices? No, according to the Jerusalem council in Acts 15. Do Jews continue to uphold the rituals and traditions that had set their community apart for centuries? Yes, according to Acts 21.

What begins to take shape is a group of believers who are united in Spirit and faith, while living out that faith in divergent ways. Jews living as Jews, Gentiles living as Gentiles, and the dividing wall between the two being torn down in the body of Messiah (Ephesians 2:14).

After all, isn't this what the long prophesied messianic era was to be all about? Israel and the nations living in harmony with one another rather than warring against each other, as we see so often throughout the pages of the Old Testament? As theologian Kendall Soulen explains, Jesus finally brings about "an economy of mutual blessing" between Jews and non-Jews, creating in his body a lasting and profound peace.[3]

But this beautiful harmony is exactly what got erased in the parting of the ways. The increasingly Gentile church adopted a zero-tolerance policy for Jews maintaining their Jewish identity (à la Ignatius), which paradoxically became antithetical to following Jesus. Meanwhile, the Jewish community—now led by the rabbis in the absence of the temple, which was destroyed by the Romans in AD 70—worked to stomp out the possibility of Jesus-believers in their midst.

After the two Jewish revolts against the Roman Empire (the first in AD 66–73, during which the temple was destroyed, and the second in AD 132–136, which ended with the Romans exiling the Jews from the city of Jerusalem), it became a liability for Gentile Christians to identify with Judaism. In fact, the main desire was to *distance* Christianity (which was becoming increasingly favorable to the Empire) from the Judaism that proved so problematic to the Romans. As is often the case with negative identity definition, those who claimed both traditions threw a wrench into the process. As time went on, neither community would tolerate them.

What we end up with is an entirely Gentile church on one hand and a Judaism that anathematizes belief in Jesus on the other. The group that becomes lost to history—for centuries—are those who confess Jesus as Jews, those who once bridged these now mutually exclusive communities.

∽·∽·∽

Despite my growing love for the Jewish rituals and worship at Ahavat Zion Messianic Synagogue in Beverly Hills, I still felt drawn to the spiritual richness of the Episcopal church. I wasn't quite ready to say goodbye to incense and stoles and partaking weekly in the Eucharist. For another full year, I attended Ahavat Zion on Saturdays and St. James' on Sundays, feeling within my body the whiplash of the parting of the ways and the yawning chasm left in its wake.

As I drove down Pico Boulevard in the heart of Jewish Los Angeles on Saturday mornings, I marveled at the throngs of religious Jews walking to synagogue. Men with long beards, black suits, and dangling tzitzit, women with long flowing skirts and brightly colored scarves covering their hair, children moving together in small groups animated by laughter and chatter. For me, it felt like a different world with its own set of insider rhythms and rules. Many of the restaurants and bakeries in the Pico-Robertson area are kosher, which means, among other things that, they are closed on Shabbat, with their owners and workers likely among those walking to one of the many neighborhood synagogues.

Having never experienced this kind of Jewish community, I felt like I had been transported to a different place or possibly a different era. I reflected anew on my own longtime desire to walk to church, and I got the sense that these Jews—who all necessarily lived within walking distance from one another and their places of worship—experienced a kind of spiritual community that I knew nothing of.

Then, a mere twenty-four hours later, I would walk through the heavy wooden double doors of St. James' Episcopal Church. Passing the white stone baptismal font, I would slip into one of the ornate pews that adorned the large sanctuary. The late morning sun filtering in through the high stained-glass windows bathed the congregation in a soft and resplendent light, truly creating the sensation of sacred space. By now I had learned the cadence of the carefully ordered service, which reached its liturgical crescendo in the communal partaking of the Eucharist.

I felt as though I was leading a double life. Did these Christians know anything of the Jewish world that existed just on the other side of the city? Did they care? Would it ever have occurred to them that Jesus may have had more in common with the Jews in West Los Angeles than the Christians here in the pews? Were there places where these two worlds, both of which I now felt some ownership of, intersected and overlapped? And where oh where was my place, my home amid these wildly different communities?

⌣·⌣·⌣

Ignatius was merely one of a whole host of voices that paved the parting of the ways. A hundred years after his stark declaration of monstrousness, Constantine would become the first "Christian" emperor in Rome. As the legend goes, on the eve of the Battle of the Milvian Bridge in AD 312, Constantine had a vision of Jesus in the sky telling him, "In my name conquer." He went on to win the battle and, in some sense, become a Christian. Soon after, the prominent theologian and church father Augustine would begin developing a Christian doctrine of just war as the beginning of a long legacy that would follow. Christianity was now coupled with power.

In AD 325, Constantine convened the Council of Nicaea, whose primary purpose was to establish an official church ruling on a doctrinal controversy that was tearing the community apart. At stake was the proper understanding of Jesus' identity—was he begotten by the Father with no beginning (as Athanasius claimed) or was he created out of nothing at some point in time (as Arius claimed)?

While many are familiar with the words of the Nicene Creed, which was drafted at this council and strongly affirms the first position, few are aware of the impact this event would have on the relationship between Judaism and Christianity. Constantine was certainly influenced by the prevailing trends of growing hostility between the mostly Gentile church and the Jewish community. In fact, he would essentially institutionalize these attitudes and effectually set them in stone.

THE NICENE CREED

We believe in one God,
the Father, the Almighty,
maker of heaven and earth,
of all that is, seen and unseen.

We believe in one Lord, Jesus Christ,
the only Son of God,
eternally begotten of the Father,
God from God, Light from Light,
true God from true God,
begotten, not made,

of one Being with the Father.

Through him all things were made.

For us and for our salvation

he came down from heaven:

by the power of the Holy Spirit

he became incarnate from the Virgin Mary,

and was made man.

For our sake he was crucified under Pontius Pilate;

he suffered death and was buried.

On the third day he rose again

in accordance with the Scriptures;

he ascended into heaven

and is seated at the right hand of the Father.

He will come again in glory to judge the living and the dead,

and his kingdom will have no end.

We believe in the Holy Spirit, the Lord, the giver of life,

who proceeds from the Father and the Son.

With the Father and the Son he is worshiped and glorified.

He has spoken through the Prophets.

We believe in one holy catholic and apostolic Church.

We acknowledge one baptism for the forgiveness of sins.

We look for the resurrection of the dead,

and the life of the world to come. Amen.

One tangible and enduring mark of this separation was the wedge that the Council of Nicaea drove between Passover and Easter. "We ought not therefore to have anything in common with the Jews, for the Savior has shown us another way," thundered Constantine. "It was declared to be particularly unworthy for this, the holiest of all festivals, to follow the calculation of the Jews, who had soiled their hands with the most fearful of crimes, and whose minds were blinded." And with that, this Christian emperor forever decoupled the Jews' remembrance of their exodus from Egypt and the resurrection of Messiah. From then on, it is a mere calendrical accident if the two happen to coincide.

So, not only did the Council of Nicaea definitively rule in favor of Athanasian Christology, it also sealed Christianity off from Judaism, both liturgically and theologically. This inaugurated a long historical era whereby, if a Jew wanted to follow Jesus as Messiah, she was required to publicly renounce any and all connections with the Jewish world. Here's an actual conversion liturgy from the seventh century:

> I do here and now renounce every rite and observance of the Jewish religion, detesting all its most solemn ceremonies and tenets that in former days I kept and held. In future I will practice no rite or celebration connected with it, nor any custom of my past error, promising neither to seek it out nor to perform it. Further do I renounce all things forbidden or detested by Christian teaching; and (recitation of the Nicene Creed).
>
> In the name of this Creed, which I truly believe and hold with all my heart, I promise that I will never return to the vomit of Jewish superstition. Never again will I fulfill any of the offices of Jewish ceremonies to which I was addicted, nor ever more hold them dear. I altogether deny and reject the errors of the Jewish religion, casting forth whatever conflicts with the Christian Faith, and affirming that my belief in the Holy Trinity is strong enough to make me live the truly Christian life, shun all intercourse with other Jews and have the circle of my friends only among honest Christians.[4]

Amazing, isn't it? No more Jewish holidays or kosher dietary practices (in fact, one's conversion was often accompanied by the public eating of pork as a sign of true devotion to Christ). No more associating with Jewish family or community. No more participating in the rituals that define the Jewish people and their corporate life and worship (and that were, by the way, commanded by God in the Old Testament). Isn't it astonishing how different this scenario is from the pages of the New Testament?

Perhaps what is most remarkable is that many Christians today give little thought to this process and the ways it has shaped Christianity. The gospel that is generally preached has very little to do with Judaism, or the Torah, or the people of Israel—except maybe in that it offers Christians a certain freedom from these things (and we wonder why so few Jews have chosen to follow Jesus!).

However, in reality, what are so often perceived as dusty Jewish concepts stood at the very heart of Jesus' gospel proclamation. For his early followers, Jesus' mission and message was absolutely incomprehensible outside the framework of God's covenant with the Jewish people and the promises that anchored that covenant. Jesus came to fulfill the promises that had been made to the people of Israel, not to replace God's chosen people with a new group. The gospel is, then, all about God's faithfulness to the covenant God made with Abraham and his descendants, and that was fleshed out through the Torah given to Moses.

Is the gospel that the church preaches today anchored in God's enduring covenant with Israel? What might it look like to increasingly tie these two stories back together? If Jesus' Jewish context is indispensable for understanding his core message, then the proclamation of the "good news" needs to affirm God's covenant faithfulness to the people of Israel, upon which God's faithfulness to the Christian church is built. If our gospel subtly but surely writes

Israel out of the narrative, how then can it be built upon Israel's Scriptures? Historically, in one way or another, the church's gospel has not translated into good news for the people of Israel. Much of what is needed today is a rethinking of our core theological categories, perhaps most centrally our gospel message.

2

THE EXCLUDED MIDDLE

*I've received a phone call from my Jewish counterpart
on the Jewish-Evangelical Dialogue. He says he has at least
three dialogue partners who are going to pull out
if we have a Messianic Jew in the meeting.*

David Neff

As we wound through the snaking curves of Malibu Canyon
Road, I found myself half engaged in a conversation about
dating with three other Fuller seminarians. All single, we be-
moaned the difficulties of dating while in seminary and the layer
of ambiguity that theology often introduced into a process that
otherwise seemed perfectly straightforward.

I listened along, smiling and nodding sympathetically, but the
other half of my attention remained stubbornly preoccupied with
worry over the in-betweenness of my identity and how it would
play out over the next twenty-four hours. My companions and I
were traveling to an annual interfaith retreat called Intersem, held
each year at a Jewish conference center nestled in the Malibu hills.

Upon exiting the canyon and rounding the final curve, the road began a slow descent and the magnificent span of the Pacific Ocean opened up before us, sparkling in the late afternoon sun. "Well, here we go," I whispered to myself, swallowing hard.

During my years as a doctoral student at Fuller Seminary, participating in different incarnations of Jewish-Christian dialogue became a mainstay of my experience. But it was never easy or uncomplicated. This was particularly true of Intersem, which was attended each year by a cohort of Fuller students. Looking back, somehow the serenity and stunning beauty of the setting highlights the incoherence and inner angst of my times spent there.

Founded in 1971, Intersem is a program in which students from several different seminaries in the Los Angeles area—representing various streams and denominations of Judaism and Christianity—gather together for twenty-four hours each January. The retreat includes shared meals, times of structured dialogue with trained facilitators, and three different worship services from Catholic, Protestant, and Jewish traditions.

The first year I attended Intersem, I had already been regularly worshiping at Ahavat Zion Messianic Synagogue and my life had become increasingly patterned around Jewish rhythms. As I began to meet the other attendees, I was reticent to share that I was both Jewish and Christian; these kinds of dialogues generally stand upon clear boundaries with no outliers. So initially, I was just "Jen from Fuller," and presumably everyone assumed I was a Protestant, evangelical Christian.

But inside, the experience was a crucible for me, highlighting the ways in which my hybrid identity was anathema to the categories that define today's religious landscape. The sharpest part of the experience was realizing how much more deeply I resonated with the Jewish worship service than either the Catholic or Protestant ones. As the Jewish seminarians sung the words of *shaharit* (the morning prayer service) accompanied by the thumping beat of a djembe drum, I found myself closing my eyes and quietly singing along. I could feel the blood of the Jewish people coursing through my veins.

ᩇ·ᩇ·ᩇ

The trajectory set by Ignatius and Constantine became the main mode of Christianity's relations with the Jewish people, and Christian anti-Judaism (all too often accompanied by acts of violence) gained momentum throughout the Middle Ages and the Protestant Reformation and into the modern era. Martin Luther, the father of the Protestant Reformation, actually became *more* anti-Semitic as his life went on.[1]

Near the end of his life, he penned a tractate called *On the Jews and Their Lies,* and here he offered a detailed account of what it means for the Jews ("a miserable, blind, and senseless people") to be the accursed and judged people of God. Citing the destruction of the Second Temple in AD 70 and the Jews' dispersion throughout the world, Luther concludes that "this work of wrath is proof that the Jews, surely rejected by God, are no longer his people, and neither is he any longer their God."

For Luther, the Jews' rejection and forsakenness by God was a result of their perpetual obstinance and evil deeds. This made them a very real threat to Christians, and one that must be vigilantly guarded against. "Therefore, dear Christian," Luther implored, "be advised and do not doubt that next to the devil, you have no more bitter, venomous, and vehement foe than a real Jew who earnestly seeks to be a Jew."[2]

The Protestant Reformation cast the mold for the next 450 years of Pauline interpretation. Luther framed his struggle against the

Catholic Church as parallel to Paul's alleged struggle against the Judaism of his day. He saw Catholicism as dry, legalistic, and corrupt, and through his eyes, this is precisely how Paul viewed Judaism. Just as Luther eventually broke away from Catholicism and dedicated himself to exposing its deep flaws, so too was Paul understood as having had a radical break with Judaism.

This narrative formed the core of Pauline scholarship until well into the twentieth century, when new perspectives on Paul began to emerge. Because of Luther's widespread influence in (especially Protestant) Christianity, his lens on Paul carried the day. But events like the Holocaust and the creation of the modern state of Israel caused Christians to scratch their heads and wonder whether the Christian tradition might have missed something with regard to its relationship with Judaism. These events drew the Jewish people onto the center stage of world history, and the church was forced to reckon with the dangerous and destructive consequences of its deep-seated negative theology of Israel and Judaism.

In the latter half of the twentieth century, New Testament scholars increasingly began to wonder whether perhaps Paul *never* had a sharp break with Judaism, and whether the juxtaposition of "grace through faith" and "works righteousness" was too blunt and inaccurate. Today, there is an entire school of Pauline scholars who commonly refer to themselves as the "Paul Within Judaism" camp, making clear that their starting point as they approach the biblical text is that Paul remained a Torah-observant Jew until the day he died. These scholars include Mark Nanos, Paula Fredriksen, Pamela Eisenbaum, Magnus Zetterholm, and Anders Runesson. Key Pauline texts take on a different hue if viewed through this lens, and the central issues that Paul was dealing with begin to take a new shape.

For example, what if passages that appear to speak negatively about the "law" (such as Romans 7:6 and Galatians 5:18) were written to Gentiles, not to Jews? What if Paul was trying to dissuade Gentile followers of Jesus from feeling it necessary to take on Jewish practice, which the Jerusalem council in Acts 15 ruled as unnecessary? Jesus had opened the door for Gentiles to be "grafted in" to God's covenant with Israel, and the New Testament is clear that they do not need to become Jews in order to do so. This is the marvel of the gospel, and yet we miss the sheer miracle of it if we assume that Paul encouraged Jews to forsake their everlasting covenant with God. Rather, Jews *as Jews* and Gentiles *as Gentiles* now together form the community of Messiah.

It is also significant that many of the scholars who are driving this new paradigm in Pauline scholarship are Jews themselves, which is why it makes perfect sense that they would read the New Testament with a different set of eyes than Gentile Christians.[3] Indeed, throughout history, many of the Christian New Testament commentators who forged the "traditional" perspective on Paul had never actually met a Jew. Rather, they employed what one scholar calls "the hermeneutical Jew" in their portraits of the New Testament and church history: Jews were used to fill a certain role in Christian theology, whether or not that portrayal accurately reflected real, living Jews.[4]

ᔕ·ᔕ·ᔕ

At my first Intersem retreat, I met Adam, a Conservative Jew. In the months that followed the retreat, Adam and I had a number of heated discussions about my identity and his reaction to it.

"Adam, all of Jesus' early followers were Jewish. They recognized him as Israel's long-awaited Messiah," I explained as we sipped lattes at The Coffee Bean & Tea Leaf.

"But Jen," retorted Adam, "every branch of Judaism agrees that Jesus was not the Messiah! We study him as one among a long list of failed messiahs. Certainly he didn't actually usher in the messianic age—just look around!"

Around and around we went. Despite our deep theological differences, Adam and I became friends and he eventually encouraged me to join the Intersem planning committee, which met monthly for six months leading up to the annual dialogue retreat. I timidly agreed, though embracing my identity in these small, intimate settings proved to be even more difficult than in the large annual retreats, where anonymity and ambiguous language were more viable options.

After the first few planning meetings, most of the Jewish students (and faculty representatives) on the planning committee knew that I was a Messianic Jew. Reactions were varied, and only a small handful of them engaged me about it, mostly in slightly skeptical but curious tones. Jews in general tend to be quite suspicious of Messianic Jews, for two main reasons: First, despite the fact that according to Jewish law, one can never cease being a Jew, Messianic Jews are often viewed as having "converted" to Christianity and thus defected from the Jewish people. Second, Messianic Judaism has a notorious history of being in-your-face evangelistic, leaving Jews with the feeling that they are not so secretly being targeted for conversion as well. Historically, a Jew entering the Christian church essentially meant the end of Jewish life and identity, a fact that makes the mere thought of conversion a threat to most Jews.

One night in September, after a lively Intersem planning meeting that took place in the *beit midrash* (Jewish study hall) at American Jewish University, the Jewish attendees wanted to draw on those present to form a *minyan* for one who was mourning a family member's death. In Judaism, grieving the loss of a loved one is a sacralized process, and reciting the designated mourner's prayers requires the presence of ten Jews (referred to as a *minyan*). Because this was a Conservative (not Orthodox) Jewish institution, women as well as men were counted in a minyan.

As fate would have it, I was the tenth Jew. They would need me to make a minyan. Messianic Jews, in many cases, are not counted in Jewish minyans, which is an intentionally exclusionary practice that highlights our general status as outsiders, apostates, and potential threats to the fabric of Jewish life.

One Jewish student pulled out her *siddur* (Jewish prayer book), ready to begin the prayers, apparently not realizing that this was a problem. A hushed murmur passed among the other students. "I'm happy to pray with you all, but I understand if it's an uncomfortable issue. Don't feel any pressure from me," I hurriedly blurted out, knowing exactly what was happening. After more whispered conversation and several apologies from the Jewish students who had become my friends, the group decided to skip the praying and everyone quickly and somewhat awkwardly dispersed into the dark parking lot. In that moment, I felt the acute sting of rejection from my own people, on account of Jesus.

The tensions did not subside. Two months later, Jim Butler, the faculty representative from Fuller, pulled me aside after the monthly planning meeting. "I want you to know that the faculty representative from one of the Jewish institutions wants to ban you from attending Intersem," he told me. "But we've been through this issue before, so don't worry. You're absolutely still going to be able to participate."

I felt frozen, unable to move. At first, I couldn't respond at all. *Is it worth it to keep being a part of Intersem with a group of people that clearly doesn't want me to be included?* I wondered, suddenly questioning the value of my presence at all. As I began to think about the relationships I had developed with the other students and how much I valued them, my eyes filled with tears.

The next day I got a call from Fuller's then president, Rich Mouw. "Jen, we had this issue come up in the past and I assured all of those involved that participation of any member of our student body is our policy for being a part of Intersem," he said reassuringly. "I'm sorry that this issue is surfacing again, and that you're having to feel the force of it."

"Thanks, Dr. Mouw, for your kind words. I've just been wondering whether it's worth it . . ." Before I could finish my sentence, Rich jumped in. "It's worth it, Jen. They need your voice in these conversations, even if it pushes some people out of their comfort zones. Of what value is interfaith dialogue if it doesn't challenge us to think differently?"

Guided by Jim and Rich, I would spend the next three years on the planning committee and attending the annual retreats. I tried to ignore the sideways glances from certain Jewish faculty members, reminding myself of Rich's wholehearted encouragement. I could even say that I became more at ease embodying my dual-identity at Intersem, though I cannot say that I was ever fully accepted as such. Though I was never actually thrown out of a synagogue, Jesus' words in John 16:2 offered me a strange kind of solace.

ഗ·ഗ·ഗ

The post-Holocaust era has been marked by deliberate efforts from Christians to bring healing and repair to the difficult history between Christians and Jews. Jews, in return, have slowly responded to this, offering theological statements that seek to revise previous stereotypes and beliefs about Christians and charting out new ways of relating to Christians. We are living in remarkable times with regard to the relationship between Christians and Jews, and there are countless efforts of dialogical engagement and partnering on shared initiatives.

Oftentimes when I teach about this significant era in my classes, I begin by reciting the Jewish *shechecheyanu* prayer, which is saved for special and momentous occasions: "*Baruch atah Adonai, Eloheinu Melech haolam, shehecheyanu, v'kiy'manu, v'higiyanu laz'man hazeh.*" (Blessed are You, Lord our God, King of the Universe, who has kept us alive, sustained us, and brought us to this season.)

The role of Messianic Jews has continually posed a curious dilemma for proponents of improved Jewish-Christian relations. Both sides have had a difficult time mapping Messianic Jews on the religious landscape, as Messianic Judaism categorically blurs the lines that the dialogue has come to depend upon. If the dialogue is about reaching across differences and gaining mutual understanding, those differences must be clearly defined.[5]

This apprehension about Messianic Jewish recognition and participation is especially evident from the Jewish side. Jewish theologian David Novak, a strong advocate for Jewish-Christian dialogue, has repeatedly noted the problematic nature of Messianic Judaism. According to Novak, Messianic Judaism fails to respect the irreducibly divergent truth claims of Judaism and Christianity, upon which authentic Jewish-Christian dialogue is built. Novak promotes honest theological engagement that does not conceal or dilute truth claims for the sake of conciliation. For Novak, the respective truth claims of Judaism and Christianity must be brought to the table if true Jewish-Christian dialogue is to take place.

In his words, "The ultimate truth claims of Judaism and Christianity are not only different but mutually exclusive. . . . One cannot live as a Jew and a Christian simultaneously." Within the framework of Novak's mutually exclusive construal of Judaism and Christianity, "the highest form of worship of the Lord God of Israel is *either* by the Torah and the tradition of the Jewish people *or* by Christ and the tradition of the Church."[6] While adherents of these two religions can seek to understand one another, such understanding is grounded in the *distinction between* the two religions. It is this boundary that, according to Novak, Messianic Judaism transgresses.

Novak's conclusions regarding Messianic Judaism follow from his understanding of Judaism and Christianity. Because Novak categorically disallows any overlap between Judaism and Christianity, Messianic Judaism cannot be anything but a syncretistic aberration that undermines and relativizes the integrity of both. Challenging his conclusions requires challenging the assumptions he makes in order to assert them.

ᔕ·ᔕ·ᔕ

"Jen, I know it's not your crowd, but I think it would be great if you could join the Evangelical-Mormon dialogue next month," my friend Cory remarked as we chatted on Fuller's campus. For Rich Mouw, interfaith dialogue stands near the center of the Christian theological task; he was among the pioneering faculty leaders in Intersem, and he had long been developing meaningful relationships with key leaders in the Church of Jesus Christ of Latter-day Saints. Cory (who was Mouw's doctoral student at the time) had also become deeply involved in these dialogues, and he knew that even though this forum wasn't exactly my wheelhouse, I too was passionate about interfaith engagement. Because I was writing on interfaith dialogue, I welcomed any opportunity to participate in meaningful dialogue across doctrinal lines. So, I agreed to attend.

It was at this dialogue that I met David Neff, who at the time was editor in chief at *Christianity Today*. We got to talking, and he began to tell me about an annual (and fairly high profile) Jewish-evangelical dialogue that took place every spring in Washington, DC. Before long, I found myself invited to the dialogue. Though I felt a bit uncomfortable about the issues that I knew were lying just under the surface, I took a deep breath, bought a plane ticket, and booked a hotel room. Maybe, for this particular group, the boundaries and the importance of maintaining them were less clearly defined.

Three months later, a mere one week before the DC event, I got an email from David Neff. "I've got bad news," it began. I held my breath and read on. "I've received a phone call from my Jewish counterpart on the Jewish-Evangelical Dialogue and he says he has at least three dialogue partners who are going to pull out if we have a Messianic Jew in the meeting. I would personally have no problem with your attending in any case, but I really don't want the dialogue to run aground on this issue. Are you willing to withdraw rather than have the dialogue fall apart? I'm really sorry to have to ask these questions, but I think the dialogue depends on it."

I was in a teaching workshop as I read David's email, and I'm pretty sure I caught nothing of the rest of the presentation. I felt shaky and exposed, like everyone in the room must be looking at me and wondering, "What is *she* doing here?" After the initial shock set in, I wrote to Mark Kinzer and David Rudolph, two of my closest Messianic Jewish friends and colleagues, and Amy-Jill Levine, a Jewish New Testament scholar who was scheduled to attend the dialogue. The next day, I wrote back to David Neff and withdrew.

While we are indeed living in remarkable times, which are yielding incredible glimpses of Jewish-Christian reconciliation, the phenomenon of the excluded middle is still strong at work. Messianic Jews are often viewed with skepticism, misunderstanding, and distrust. Much of this has to do with the checkered history of the Messianic Jewish movement, but it is also on account of both Judaism and Christianity's attraction to clear boundaries and bounded sets.

As missiologist Paul Hiebert explains, bounded sets represent clear-cut categories whose distinctions are black and white. So, for example, we could have apples and oranges; each is defined by its static, essential characteristics which distinguish it from the other. Something cannot be 70 percent apple and 30 percent orange. In defining what an apple is, we are also defining what it is *not*. This type of thinking and categorizing often gets projected onto religious groups, a practice that missiologists in particular are increasingly critiquing.

By contrast, a centered set defines objects or groups by their relationship to a designated center. Boundaries, then, are less of the main focus, and there is room for a certain fluidity and dynamic mode of defining. Within centered sets "each object must be considered individually. It is not reduced to a single common uniformity within the category."[7]

If Jewish-Christian dialogue is to proceed along a bounded-set model, then Messianic Judaism will continue to pose problems. However, if the categories themselves can be challenged, new possibilities emerge. While Christians and Jews may disagree on key theological doctrines, an honest look at history reveals that the categories we often take for granted are not quite as stable as we might assume. In fact, according to some, they were artificially manufactured for the express purpose of defining who's in and who's out.[8] If the parting of the ways is seen as a mutual process of Judaism and Christianity distancing themselves from one another—and not some kind of inevitable division based on core differences—we just may find ourselves rethinking the differences that once seemed absolute.

3

LOST IN TRANSLATION

Just then a woman, losing blood for twelve years, came from
behind and touched the tzitzit *of His garment. For she kept saying*
to herself, "If only I touch His garment, I will be healed."

MATTHEW 9:20-21 TLV

I parked in a metered parking spot along Beverly Drive, adjusted
my skirt, and walked into the lobby of the Beverly Hills Marriott.
I had only been attending Ahavat Zion Messianic Synagogue for a
few months, and I continued to be intimidated by the unfamiliar
faces and the rhythms of worship, which were still foreign to me.
Though I had a fairly strong sense of my Jewish identity growing
up, the fact that we were never involved in a Jewish community left
me with a steep learning curve.

I'd decided to attend the Messianic Jewish conference that the
synagogue was hosting as I was curious to meet other Jewish followers of Jesus and share stories with them. As much as I was pursuing the path of my spiritual journey, it felt as though it was equally
persistently pursuing me. The people I had met, books I had read,[1]

and the experiences I was having were all landmarks along the way, and this conference seemed to be the next step.

I stepped into the elevator and got off on the second floor, trying to find my way to the conference room where the sessions were being held. I was a few minutes late, and as I walked down the hallway I could hear the songs of shaharit; the group had already begun the traditional Jewish morning prayers. As I rounded the final turn and reached the conference room, I was stunned to see someone who looked a lot like my friend Jonathan, but I barely recognized him.

He was wearing a flowing black and white *tallit* (Jewish prayer shawl), and his head and left arm were adorned with the leather straps of *tefillin* (phylacteries), which I had never seen before. They are not worn on Shabbat, so despite my recent attendance at Ahavat Zion, I was completely dumbfounded about what they were. (If you also have never seen tefillin, you should Google images of Jews praying with them. Then you will understand my confusion.) Much later, my aunt would remark that a Jew wearing tefillin looks like a ninja.

I smiled timidly, feeling disoriented that this person wrapped in leather straps was indeed my friend Jonathan, and he kindly ushered me into the room. Sure enough, all of the other men were wrapped up as well. Acting like this was normal to me, I chose an aisle seat, pulled out my siddur and began to follow along. Mostly, I pretended I was looking at the pages in front of me while actually glancing sideways at the leather-bound men (and a few women, too) on either side of me.

As I would later learn, the practice of "laying tefillin" during weekday morning prayers is how Jewish tradition came to interpret and apply verses such as Deuteronomy 6:8, where God commands the Israelites to tie the commandments "as symbols on your hands and bind them on your foreheads." Tefillin are fitted with small leather boxes that are affixed with leather straps to one's forehead and arm, and inside of the boxes are tiny scrolls bearing the words of the four verses that reference the practice.[2] Tefillin are thus a powerful reminder of the deeply embodied nature of Judaism.

Lest we believe that the idea of tefillin is obscure and marginal, Deuteronomy 6:4-9 is in fact one of the most central texts in all of Judaism. It begins with the ever-meaningful opening verse of the *Shema* ("Hear O Israel, the LORD our God, the LORD is one" TLV), Judaism's central declaration of the oneness of God. Religious Jews recite this passage in prayer three times a day and have it on their lips during their last moments of life.

Throughout the conference my mind was swirling, and it turned out to be yet another important step in my journey back to Judaism. The embodied nature of Jewish spirituality, the infectious melodies of Jewish prayer, the impassioned pleas in the siddur that reveal the Jewish people's intimate relationship with God; in the weeks following the conference, all of it continued to seep in. There is something beautiful and mysterious about the Jewish people and their winding and complex story of peoplehood, and I knew that I was taking steps that led me further into that profound mystery.

ഗ•ഗ•ഗ

Along with tefillin, one engaged in Jewish prayer dons a fringed garment called a tallit. Also biblical, this practice originates from Numbers 15:37-41, where God commands the Israelites to "make for themselves tassels on the corners of their garments . . . so that you may remember to do all my commandments and be holy to your God" (author's translation). The Hebrew word here is *tzitzit*, and the imagery is that of covering oneself with the word of God, a physical and embodied reminder of the nearness of God and his tangible presence in our world.

The idea is that by looking upon the fringes, we will be reminded to follow God and his ways rather than the other paths that clamor for our allegiance. While the donning of a tallit may not be as visually striking or unfamiliar as laying tefillin, the two practices are closely bound together in that they are part and parcel of Jewish prayer.

Jesus, too, wore this fringed garment. Our English Bibles, however, don't make this little detail particularly clear. Look, for example, at Matthew 9. The context of this chapter is striking, which we will discuss more in the next chapter. For now, let's focus on verse 20. The woman with the problem of bleeding reaches out to Jesus and touches "the edge of his cloak."[3] Cloak? Is he Gandalf?

What the Greek actually says is that she reaches out and touches the *kraspedon* (literally, tassels or fringes) of his garment. Ah, that's interesting. Tassels. Just like the tassels commanded in Numbers 15. The same word is used in the parallel passage in Luke 8:44, as well as in Matthew 14:36 (and, parallel, Mark 6:56) where the sick are healed by touching the tassels on Jesus' garment. In each of these instances, most English translations say "hem" or "edge" of his cloak or garment.

However, when the same Greek word (*kraspedon*) appears in Matthew 23:5—where Jesus is censuring the Pharisees for their showiness—the word tassel is used.[4] See what's happening? Our English Bibles would have us believe that those hypocritical and "legalistic" Pharisees wear tassels, but Jesus Gandalf wears a cloak. What often gets missed is that *this is the exact same word*.

This is merely one instance in which the English translation serves to obscure Jesus' connection to Jewish practices and distance Jesus from the customs of the Pharisees. In reality, wearing tassels was (and is) common Jewish practice—that Jesus and the Pharisees *both* adhered to. As my friend Matthew Thiessen writes, Jesus was indeed "*that* Jewish."[5]

Jewish practices, such as wearing tassels, embed Jesus in a particular context. Understanding this context is the key to understanding the significance of his life and actions.

ᴄᴧ·ᴄᴧ·ᴄᴧ

A few months after the conference in Beverly Hills, I found myself back in neighboring Bel Air to attend a lecture by Jewish New Testament scholar Mark Nanos. Nanos is among an emerging group of Jewish scholars who are prompting the academic world to reconsider common assumptions about the New Testament, particularly with regard to the Jewishness of Jesus, Paul, and the early Jesus-believing community.

At this particular lecture, Nanos unpacked the way he reads Romans 11:17, the beginning of Paul's enigmatic "grafting in" passage. Romans 9–11 are Paul's musings on God's faithfulness to the people of Israel which, in previous generations of New Testament scholarship, seemed to be merely extraneous material oddly inserted into a letter about sin and Christ's salvific grace. Now, however, scholars are increasingly seeing these three chapters as the *key to unlocking the meaning of the entire book.*

Most English Bibles translate Romans 11:17 as some branches being "broken off," an image that suggests that those branches have been pruned and severed from the root. The implication here is that Israel's covenant with God has been fundamentally ruptured on account of Israel's unbelief in Jesus. This verse has all too often been used to fuel the Christian narrative that Israel is the ex-wife of God and the Christian church is God's much younger new wife. In fact, replacement imagery is often embedded into English translations. The New Revised Standard Version, for example, states explicitly that the "wild olive shoot" has been grafted "in their place," as if to suggest that Gentiles are now taking the place of Israel within the covenant.

Nanos, however, explained that the Greek verb *exeklasthēsan* used in verse 17 can also be rendered as "bent," not "broken off."[6] This imagery more accurately reflects the process of grafting in, as he unpacked in his lecture. Accordingly, the "wild olive shoot" is grafted in *among* the existing branches, not in place of them. Remarkable how just a few words, translated differently, shift the whole metaphor!

According to Nanos's reading, the "natural branches" (i.e., Israel) are *bent back* in order to make room for the "wild olive shoot" (i.e., the Gentiles) to be grafted in among them. Rather than this passage being about Israel getting jettisoned from the covenant that Gentile Christians now cozily inhabit, it is a passage about how Gentile Christians, through Messiah, are invited to share in the richness of Israel's enduring covenant with God.

Nanos went on to explain how this portrait fits much more easily with Paul's other metaphors and statements, making his theology more coherent and consistent. It should also be noted that this reading helps eliminate the gap often perceived between the Paul of Acts and the Paul of his letters. In Acts 21, Paul undergoes temple purification rites to ward off rumors that he taught Jewish followers of Jesus to abrogate Jewish practice, and in Acts 23, Paul identifies himself (present tense) as a Pharisee.

For some, these passages are difficult to make sense of given some of Paul's statements in his letters, particularly his apparent negativity toward the "law." To resolve this tension, many scholars dismiss the book of Acts as "not historical" (and thus somehow not authoritative), while others conclude that Acts is merely Luke's depiction of Paul (and thus somehow not accurate). According to

Nanos, however, the problem is not with the Paul of Acts but with the way we have historically translated and interpreted his letters! Despite all of this, I have yet to see an English translation that reflects Nanos's argument and conclusions.[7]

What we see here is that our reading of Scripture is never done in a vacuum. Indeed, we bring our own set of lenses to the text, and the translations we read often serve to reinforce our presuppositions and assumptions. While the Bible shapes our theology in profound ways, Christian theology throughout the centuries has also shaped the Bible, and the way it gets read. The parting of the ways between Judaism and Christianity has become one of the ingrained lenses through which we read our Bibles.

In her book *The Misunderstood Jew: The Church and the Scandal of the Jewish Jesus*, Jewish New Testament scholar Amy-Jill Levine describes the way in which the Christian tradition has historically portrayed Jesus vis-à-vis Judaism. In her words, Jesus is

> Defined, incorrectly and unfortunately, as "against" the Law . . . ; as "against" the Temple . . . ; [and] as "against" the people Israel . . . Judaism becomes in such discourse a negative foil: whatever Jesus stands for, Judaism isn't it; whatever Jesus is against, Judaism epitomizes the category. No wonder even today Jesus somehow looks "different" from "the Jews": in the movies and artistic renderings, he's blond and they are swarthy; he is cute and buff and they need rhinoplasty and Pilates. Jesus and his followers such as Peter and Mary Magdalene become identified as (proto-)Christian; only those who chose not to follow him remain "Jews."[8]

As the translation decisions in Romans 11 make clear, Paul has been portrayed similarly. It is no wonder that most Jews today (and throughout history) do not recognize Jesus as one of their own, and worse yet, want nothing to do with him.

ↄ·ↄ·ↄ

What's at stake in the issue of Bible translation? First, we need to take account of the way history has shaped our reading of Scripture. In this case, special attention needs to be paid to the parting of the ways between Judaism and Christianity. Once Judaism and Christianity become two separate and mutually exclusive religious systems, each tradition works hard to highlight their differences and their incompatibilities. Our biblical translations reflect this embedded agenda, and import meaning that simply did not exist in the text's original rendering. Surfacing and naming this agenda is part of reading the Bible well, and correcting it is the task of the Christian church.

In general, the default perspective today is to conceive of Judaism and Christianity as two entirely different (and mutually incompatible) religious traditions. While this is certainly the story history has told, *it is not reflected in the New Testament*. In fact, the New Testament is all about people living as Jews and Christians simultaneously. But if we allow history to color our reading of the text, we can easily miss this powerful reality.

Moreover, history has shown that Christianity without Judaism leads to Christianity *against* Judaism (and the Jewish people). As we saw with Martin Luther, Christianity has a long and dark history of anti-Judaism, and the past few centuries have demonstrated that it is a very short ride from anti-Judaism to anti-Semitism. While I would not consider Hitler to be a Christian in any sense of the word, it is significant that he twisted Christian theology to accomplish his aims, using Luther as an ally and champion of his cause.[9]

This fact should shake us to the very core, since Luther's words, which were used to justify Nazi concentration camps, also help form and maintain the foundation of Protestant Christian tradition. And so, we must ask: What doctrines do we believe, what lessons do we preach, what rituals do we promote that actually perpetuate anti-Judaism and anti-Semitism in subtle, covert ways? In short, how we read our Bibles *matters*.

Second, the small and seldom recognized detail that Jesus wore tzitzit (and tefillin?) offers us an opportunity to reflect on embodied practices and what it might mean to ground our own spirituality in our bodies. The Greco-Roman heritage has bequeathed to the West the sense that our bodies are working against us, that we'd be better off without them. More troubling still, certain biblical passages (such as Romans 7:21-24) seem to confirm this mentality. And yet, our bodies are the only place we have to live out our faith. It is with our hands that we lift up the needy, with our voices that we declare God's goodness, and with our mouths that we partake in the richness of Jesus' body and blood.

It is in our bodies that we are made in the image of God. If Jesus found human flesh suitable to inhabit, we have much to learn about engaging our bodies in worship and discipleship. In the words of Dallas Willard, "Our body is a primary *resource* for the spiritual life," which is why he pleads with the Christian community to "place the disciplines for the spiritual life at the heart of the gospel."[10] In other words, our faith *must* be lived out through our bodies; to overlook or ignore this reality is to miss what the gospel is all about.

Finally, we must increasingly develop the practice of reading the Bible as a *coherent whole*. Figures like Andy Stanley would have us "dispense with the old and embrace the new," making clear that the "old" is all about "legalism, hypocrisy, self-righteousness, and exclusivity."[11] I beg to differ.

The Bible, from Genesis to Revelation, is God's gift to God's people, a witness to the incredible story of God's engagement with and concern for shaping a people to make God known in the world. From *this* standpoint, we must do the hard work of teasing out how the Bible is indeed one continuous and consistent narrative. The covenant that God makes with the people of Israel reaches its apex in the person of Jesus—Israel's Messiah—and through him extends to all nations.

That Jesus is Jewish *matters*; Jesus came as the climax of a particular story with a particular people, and *that* story and people continues to matter to God. When we lose sight of this sense of continuity, we risk cutting ourselves off from the story God is continuing to tell. As Amy-Jill Levine writes, "If you get the Jewish context wrong, you will certainly get Jesus wrong."[12]

It is all too common in the Christian world to juxtapose the Old Testament (which is often seen as detailing the constant failings of a faithless people who live under a harsh and punitive system of "law") and the New Testament (which represents a mode of divine grace and unconditional love that is perceived as foreign to God's dealings with the people of Israel). Within this paradigm, the church is often conceived of as the new Israel, and God's everlasting covenant with the Jewish people is at best irrelevant and at worst annulled.

Such a framework raises serious questions about how deep God's faithfulness runs, and what this might mean for an oft-blundering church. If Israel's covenant with God is abrogated on account of Israel's rejecting Jesus, could God also abolish his covenant with the church? Is God an unreliable boyfriend with a fear of commitment? If he ditched his past love, how do Christians know that his faithfulness can be trusted? In short, the very character of God is at stake.

4

JESUS AND RITUAL PURITY

But then Yeshua *turned and saw her.*
"Take heart, daughter," He said, "your faith has made you well."
That very hour the woman was healed.

<small>MATTHEW 9:22 TLV</small>

As the plane gained altitude, I leaned back in my seat and bent open the spine of my designated travel book. I love everything about travel days: the sense of being in between, in no particular place at all; the fact there's no other place I'm supposed to be and nothing else I'm supposed to be doing; the people-watching and airport-wandering and wanderlust-indulging. As a general rule, I avoid doing work on travel days if at all possible. The liminal time and space are too precious; I've always opted for pleasure reading, especially books that easily draw me in and which I can dedicate the whole day to reading.

I was traveling to Boston to speak at a Messianic Jewish women's conference. Since I had increasingly begun to self-identify as a Messianic Jew, opportunities began to present themselves for speaking and teaching. After all, Messianic Jewish women in PhD programs are not so easy to come by. This particular conference was organized by Mark Kinzer's wife, Roz, who had become a close friend and invited me to speak. Again, it seemed like a fitting next step in my journey.

My book for this specific travel day was A. J. Jacobs's *The Year of Living Biblically*, and it was only a matter of minutes before I was literally laughing out loud, garnering strange looks and some warm smiles from fellow passengers. As the premise for the book, Jacobs attempts to spend a year following the Bible as literally as possible, chronicling his journey with diary-like entries that each focus on one specific biblical commandment. Amid an awkward sense of embarrassment, I wanted to launch a spontaneous airplane read aloud—the content was just *so* funny, I felt like it should be shared.

Jacobs's escapades with mixed fabrics, stoning Sabbath-breakers, handling serpents, and honoring widows are enthralling and often sidesplitting.[1] In one entry, he explains his attempt to avoid the ritual impurity associated with genital discharges while his wife is menstruating (see Leviticus 15:19). Unamused, she makes it a point to sit in every chair in the house before he returns home. Ultimately, he opts for a portable Handy Seat, because, really, who can be sure who might have just sat in any particular subway seat or restaurant booth?[2]

Part of the reason this story is so humorous to us is because of its utter absurdity, especially according to our modern Western worldview and our go-to lens for interpreting Scripture. In our day and age, it is wildly inappropriate to act differently—or even ask—if a woman is menstruating. And, usually unconsciously, many of us read our worldview back into Scripture.

It is easy to overlook or disregard that, in the Bible, issues of ritual purity *matter*. In his book, *Jesus and the Forces of Death: The*

Gospels' Portrayal of Ritual Impurity Within First-Century Judaism, New Testament scholar Matthew Thiessen demonstrates that ritual purity—far from being some legalistic and archaic Old Testament oddity—deeply mattered to Jesus as well. In fact, reading the Gospels through the lens of ritual purity unlocks a whole new understanding of what Jesus' ministry was all about and how it connects his life and mission to God's ongoing covenant with the people of Israel.

∽·∽·∽

Let's revisit Matthew 9:18-26. Here we have one story about a synagogue leader whose daughter has died that gets abruptly interrupted by another story about a woman who has been "subject to bleeding" for twelve years. The very language of our English translations serves to obscure key aspects of this passage that connect it to a first-century Jewish context. The stories seem to have nothing to do with each other, making the composition of the passage appear odd and haphazard. It is precisely an understanding of the ritual purity system, and Jesus' disposition toward it, that uncovers the meaning of this curious passage.

First, some background. As Thiessen explains, ancient Israel's existence is structured around two binaries: holy versus profane/ordinary, and pure versus impure. The primary loci of holiness are the Sabbath (see Exodus 20:8-11), the tabernacle/temple (see Exodus 40:34-38), and the people of Israel themselves (see Exodus 19:6, Leviticus 20:26). Because God literally *dwells* in these entities, they must be guarded and stewarded in a particular way.

We need to go all the way back to Genesis to further unpack the concept of holiness for the people of Israel. In the Genesis creation narrative, we are told six times that God beholds what he has made and calls it "good," and finds the whole of his creation "very good."

However, the climax of the narrative comes not on the sixth day (i.e., creation's completion), but on the seventh day (i.e., the blessing and sanctification of the Sabbath). While creation is repeatedly called *good*, the word *holy* only appears with reference to the Sabbath, and this is the only time the word holy appears in the entire book of Genesis.[3]

As we follow the narrative forward, we see in Exodus that the redeemed and delivered people of Israel are commissioned to be a "kingdom of priests and a holy nation" (Exodus 19:6). The holiness associated with the Sabbath gains fuller clarity through the calling and shaping of the people of Israel. The holy people are fittingly commanded to observe the Sabbath, the holy day (Exodus 20:8). Likewise, as the nation commissioned to usher the divine presence into creation, Israel is eventually tasked with building God's earthly abode, that is, the tabernacle and later the temple. The Sabbath as sanctified time and the tabernacle/temple as sanctified space are closely correlated; effectually, the Sabbath is a "temple in time" just as the temple is a "Sabbath in space."[4]

Within this framework, Israel's story and covenantal life reflect two curiously opposed threads: on one hand, Israel must carefully preserve its own holiness (and thus properly address issues of ritual impurity) and on the other hand, Scripture (especially the prophetic books) gestures toward an overflowing outward expansion of that holiness.

The juxtaposition between these two threads reminds me of a sermon I once heard, preached by my friend and colleague Scott Cormode, on the always-flowing fountains in Rome, whose water is ever-available for all to come and drink. Rather than clean water being a scarce resource that must be carefully rationed and apportioned, there is a certain extravagance about the fountains' prodigality. The holiness entrusted to Israel connotes a precious resource that Israel must stand guard to protect, while the prophetic vision is analogous to Rome's boundlessly flowing fountains.

The purity system provides the nuts and bolts of stewarding and safeguarding God's tangible presence, which the Israelites are commanded to do according to the first thread of Israel's narrative. Though the categories are not entirely precise, Thiessen and others divide biblical impurity into *ritual* and *moral*. Moral impurity refers to sinful behavior (idolatry, incest, murder, etc.), which results in defilement of the people, the sanctuary, and the land. Moral impurity is avoidable, willful, noncommunicable, incites divine chastisement, requires atonement, and, unabated, leads to exile.

Ritual impurity, by contrast, is a (generally) temporary condition that results from contact with natural and unavoidable sources of impurity. Ritual impurity is transmittable, and it is overcome by "washing and waiting," that is, ritual bathing and time. It is not sinful unless one refuses to undergo the prescribed purification procedures.

Ritual impurity falls into three main categories: skin diseases (*tsara'at* in Hebrew, *lepra* in Greek, often mistranslated as leprosy, which it most definitely was not), genital discharges, and corpses. As Thiessen explains, each of these in their own way represents the forces of death, powers that work against human life and flourishing. Problems arise if one in a state of ritual impurity comes into contact with God's holiness; God flees from impurity, as we see in Ezekiel 10.

So, while ritual impurity is not in itself sinful, not dealing with it properly can lead one into the realm of sin—and drive away God's presence. Hence Leviticus 15:31: "You must keep the Israelites separate from things that make them unclean, so they will not die in their uncleanness for defiling my dwelling place, which is among them." Israel's sanctity relies on the people's ability to guard, preserve, and carefully steward God's presence in their midst.

However, according to the second thread we see throughout the Old Testament, the holiness of God that dwells within Israel will *expand outward* into the ordinary world beyond. Ultimately, God's holiness in the midst of Israel, the Sabbath and the tabernacle/temple points forward to the final consummation of creation—God's unrestricted presence and the definitive removal of the secular/holy barrier. Jewish tradition describes the world to come as "a day that will be entirely Sabbath,"[5] and Scripture (perhaps most notably Zechariah 14 and Revelation 21) offers an eschatological vision in which God's holiness blankets all of space and time.

This trajectory is present from the very beginning, originating in God's call of Abram ("All peoples on earth will be blessed through you," Genesis 12:3), and is repeatedly echoed throughout the prophetic literature. Isaiah imagines a day when "the earth will be filled with the knowledge of the LORD as the waters cover the sea" (Isaiah 11:9) and declares that "I will also make you a light for the Gentiles, that my salvation may reach to the ends of the earth" (Isaiah 49:6). Zechariah 14 envisions a day on which the most mundane objects will be just as holy as the temple instruments in Jerusalem.

In the narrative of the Hebrew Scriptures, Israel's guarded holiness coexists with the vision that one day—"on that day"—God's presence will flow far beyond these prescribed boundaries and parameters.

⌒•⌒•⌒

So, how does all of this relate to Jesus? First, it now becomes clear that Matthew 9:18-26 (and its parallel passages, Luke 8:41-56 and Mark 5:22-43) is focused on issues of ritual purity. What the English translation subtly conceals is that the woman's "bleeding" is an issue of abnormal genital discharge, which has rendered her impure (and thus unable to enter the temple courts, and possibly the city of Jerusalem) for its entire duration. What a loss, given the Jerusalem temple's significance for worship and religious life!

What are we to make of this woman *touching* Jesus' tassels? According to the laws of ritual purity, such contact *should* have resulted in Jesus entering into a state of ritual impurity. In reality, the exact opposite happens. Rather than her impurity transferring to him, he restores her to a state of ritual purity.

Similarly, the synagogue leader's daughter represents corpse impurity and thus another force opposing Israel's life and well-being. And again, this portion of the passage is rife with touch language. In Matthew 9:18, the synagogue leader beckons Jesus to come "put his hand" on his daughter, who has just died. When Jesus finally reaches his house, Jesus raises his daughter by "taking her by the hand" (Matthew 9:25 author's translation).

As if to prepare us for this episode, Jesus' healing of a man with lepra precedes this passage in all three Synoptic Gospels. There it is: Jesus confronting all three main sources of ritual impurity in the Gospels' unfolding story of his extraordinary ministry.

In Matthew, the healing of the man with lepra is recounted in Matthew 8:1-4, and it is notably the first recorded miracle in Matthew's Gospel (and, therefore, in the entire New Testament!). While Jesus' healings do not have a standard format, Matthew is intentional to note that, in this case, he "reached out his hand and touched the man" (Matthew 8:3).

Again, according to the Levitical purity system, this action should have resulted in Jesus contracting the man's ritual impurity. However, in what must have been a shocking and scandalous surprise for Jesus' Jewish onlookers, Jesus' holiness and purity flows *outward* and heals the man; in him, God's holiness is beginning to expand outward. Once the man is healed, Jesus commands him to follow the purification ritual specified in Leviticus 14. This detail makes it clear that Jesus wasn't disregarding the purity system and its intricacies; he was working within its parameters even as he was introducing something strikingly new.

Ritual purity was a cornerstone of Second Temple Jewish life, and Jesus' actions reveal that he embodies a kind of *contagious holiness* that overcomes the sources of impurity that contaminate God's people. Without understanding how the ritual purity system works, and how Jesus' actions evidence the inbreaking of God's holiness into the world, we miss part of the New Testament's remarkable witness.

With the Covid-19 pandemic imprinted in the minds and experiences of the entire global population, the notion of contagious holiness takes on vivid significance. While ritual impurities are certainly not the same as a life-threatening virus, it's powerful to imagine what it might look like for close contact to transmit healing rather than sickness. In a world where "social distancing" became an uninvited phrase in our everyday vocabulary, Jesus' healing touch offers a beautiful antidote to the fear and anxiety that human contact has increasingly come to evoke.

Matthew is showing us that the tension between Israel's divinely commanded separateness (or guardedness) and Israel's vocation to bring God's holiness to the ends of the earth finds its resolution in the life and work of Jesus. In him, holiness overpowers the sources of impurity; abundant life overpowers the forces of death. The kingdom of God is breaking in, and *this is what it looks like*. Understanding the purity system gives us language for understanding how God's incarnation in Jesus represents both the continuation of God's story with Israel and a radically new chapter in that story.

As demonstrated by his life and ministry, Jesus embodies a "concentrated and intensified form of the divine presence,"[6] which is made especially evident through the *invasive* quality of his holiness. While contact with ritually unclean objects and persons threatened to defile Israel's holiness, Jesus' holiness flows *outward* into the impure world. Through him, the holiness embodied by Israel begins to ripple throughout creation, as it was always intended to do.

∽·∽·∽

This theme continues in the following chapters of Matthew's Gospel. When asked to authenticate his ministry and messiahship in Matthew 11, Jesus does so by pointing to what can be *seen and heard* as a result of his work. Echoing Isaiah 61, Jesus declares that "the blind receive sight, the lame walk, those who have leprosy [lepra] are cleansed, the deaf hear, the dead are raised, and the good news is proclaimed to the poor" (Matthew 11:5). His identity is confirmed by the tangible, physical restoration that, through him, is spreading outward into the world.

While Western Christianity often has us living out our faith in a way that bifurcates our "bodies" and our "spirits," this division is completely foreign to a Hebraic worldview. Judaism has always been an embodied spirituality, where we live out our faith through our bodies, not in some kind of war against them. Indeed, faith is what Jews *see and hear* (and also eat, don't eat, wear, recite, declare, and on the holiday of Sukkot, shake).

Perhaps most significant for us as followers of Jesus today is Jesus' charge to his disciples in Matthew 10. What exactly does Jesus send his first followers out to do? "As you go, proclaim this message: 'The kingdom of heaven has come near.' Heal the sick, raise the dead, cleanse those who have leprosy [lepra], drive out demons. Freely you have received; freely give" (Matthew 10:7-8). This commission understandably makes many of us uncomfortable. After all, when is the last time you raised someone from the dead?

Like Jesus, we too are to fight against the tangible forces of death in our culture. In a world with no temple, we need to do some translation work as to what this looks like in our context. What are the forces of death in our society? What factors work to oppress God's people and work against the inbreaking of God's glorious kingdom in our lives and communities? My guess is that, as we ponder these questions, a whole host of responses come to mind. The downcast, the disadvantaged, the downtrodden, the defeated— "the least of these"—these are the people who are most susceptible to catch Jesus' contagious holiness. Indeed, in the kingdom of God, strength is often disguised as weakness and pride constructs a barrier to holy encounter.

Finally, it should not be overlooked that the passages from Matthew 8–11 just reviewed immediately follow the Sermon on the Mount (Matthew 5–7). Jesus' entire discourse in this section is framed by his words in Matthew 5:17-20:

> Do not think that I have come to abolish the Law [Torah] or the Prophets; I have not come to abolish them but to fulfill them. For truly I tell you, until heaven and earth disappear, not the smallest letter, not the least stroke of a pen, will by any means disappear from the Law [Torah] until everything is accomplished. Therefore anyone who sets aside one of the least of these commands and teaches others accordingly will be called least in the kingdom of heaven, but whoever practices and teaches these commands will be called great in the kingdom of heaven. For I tell you that unless your righteousness surpasses that of the Pharisees and the teachers of the law, you will certainly not enter the kingdom of heaven.

This description makes it clear that Jesus' fulfillment of the outward expansion of Israel's holiness does *not* imply a casting away of God's covenant with Israel and its particular parameters. Jesus is the climax and continuation of God's story with Israel, not a new story altogether. It is precisely Jesus' Jewishness—his participation in and embodiment of the people of Israel—that reveals to us what his mission was all about, and in turn, what our commission as his disciples is to look like.

∽·∽·∽

My time in Boston ended up being deeply meaningful and spiritually refreshing, and the talk that I gave broached the issues we are discussing here from a different angle. I talked about the way in which Jesus determinatively overcomes the barrier between Jew and Gentile, a barrier that seems absolute in some Old Testament passages but quite permeable in other passages (mirroring the two different threads discussed above).

So many of the rather obscure laws that we read of in the Torah reinforce the theme of *distinction*. In Leviticus 19:19, the assembly of Israel is instructed not to mate different kinds of animals, not to plant their fields with two different kinds of seed, and not to wear clothing woven of two kinds of material. While there are different interpretations of what these commands were about and what they mean, one thing is clear—God values distinction and separation.

The distinction between Israel and the nations is perhaps the primary distinction which all the others simply echo and reinforce. The *Havdalah* liturgy (which Jews recite at the end of Shabbat each week) reflects this idea of distinction: "Blessed are You, Lord our God, King of the Universe, who distinguishes between sacred and secular, between light and darkness, between Israel and the nations, between the seventh day and the six days of work. Blessed are You, Lord, who distinguishes between sacred and secular."[7]

Through an Old Testament holiness lens, the distinction between Israel and "the nations" (i.e., everyone else) makes sense when we remember that only Israel worshiped the one true God, while every other people group worshiped idols. The Old Testament narrative repeatedly illustrates the way in which becoming overly intertwined with other peoples tends to drag Israel away from worshiping God. Similarly, these "nations" are also those who continually try to thwart God's promises for Israel to flourish and dwell safely in her apportioned land.

Many assume that this distinction was simply done away with in the New Testament. After all, doesn't Paul say in Galatians 3:28 that "there is neither Jew nor Greek . . . for you are all one in Christ Jesus" (ESV)? And yet, to conclude that distinction is erased is to ignore another prominent New Testament thread according to which the early Jesus-following movement is all about the *reconciliation* between Jew and Gentile. No longer do "the nations" drag Israel away from true worship of God—rather, they join Israel in that worship! After all, in the same verse just quoted, Paul also declares that there is no longer "male and female," yet his writing in other places clearly affirms that distinction between men and women endures.

With the coming of Jesus, Jews and Gentiles together worship the one true God. Side by side, in unity, Jews and Gentiles are ambassadors of Christ's outwardly expanding holiness. The distinction between Israel and the nations endures, but it looks different. It is no longer tantamount to division, strife, or hierarchy. Fidelity to God no longer looks like Israel separating itself from the surrounding nations; now, Israel gets to partner with those nations in ushering in God's kingdom.

After all, this is the reality prophesied long ago: "In that day Israel will be the third, along with Egypt and Assyria, a blessing on the earth. The LORD Almighty will bless them, saying, 'Blessed be Egypt my people, Assyria my handiwork, and Israel my inheritance'" (Isaiah 19:24-25). This vision is all the more poignant when we remember that it was from the Egyptians' mighty and merciless hands that God wrested the people of Israel in the book of Exodus, and, much later, the Assyrians were the ones who conquered the Northern Kingdom of Israel and dispersed the ten tribes who dwelt there.

As I explained in Boston, we see this shift displayed powerfully in another New Testament passage that traverses the territory of Old Testament purity: Peter's vision in Acts 10. At face value, Peter's vision appears to be about eating nonkosher animals (which, notably, he had *never* done—even since becoming a prominent follower of Jesus!). And so, many flatly conclude that with the coming of Jesus, kosher dietary laws are done away with.

However, how exactly does Peter interpret the vision in both Acts 11 and Acts 15? As it turns out, it's not about food at all; rather, it's about *Jews associating with Gentiles*. It's about the Spirit of God falling upon Gentiles in the same way the Spirit fell upon Jews in Acts 2. It's about intimate fellowship-amid-distinction, a key marker of the New Testament community of Messiah.

In some cases, Christian biblical interpretation glosses over key issues that become apparent once we view the text through the lens of its Jewish context. A misunderstanding of Jesus' relationship to ritual purity can lead us to believe that he simply disregarded the entire system, thus obscuring the much more powerful mode in which he was actually interacting with it. Similarly, a flat reading of Acts and Paul's letters can lead to the conclusion that the New Testament bluntly erases key themes from the Old Testament.

As Thiessen explains, when Jesus disagrees with or pushes back against other Jewish authority figures of his day, we are quick to assume that he was wholesale casting Judaism aside and founding a new thing called Christianity. However, to do so is to disregard the reality that Judaism has always been about Jews arguing over how to properly apply and interpret the word and commands of God. There's an old saying, "Two Jews, three opinions," and it is quite true of Jewish existence throughout the centuries and today. In this regard, a proper understanding of Judaism enables us to reimagine Jesus' relationship to it; he wasn't doing away with it, he was showing how, through him, Judaism was being brought forward in the way the prophets foretold. The events that figures like Isaiah could only imagine and pray for were now becoming a reality.

5

"THE LAND I WILL SHOW YOU"

He will raise a banner for the nations
and gather the exiles of Israel; he will assemble the scattered people
of Judah from the four quarters of the earth.

ISAIAH 11:12

It was December 2007, and I sat in the lobby of the Jerusalem Gold Hotel, waiting to meet Rabbi Stein in person for the first time. Our group would be heading to Ben Gurion airport in a few hours, where we would board a plane back to the US after having spent a head-spinning ten days in Israel. My mind was swirling and as I stared out the window into the parking lot, images from our trip played across my mind.

The sand-colored stone walls surrounding the Old City of Jerusalem, the grassy green hills of the Galilee, the shimmering expanse of the Mediterranean Sea. The sky-high mystical town of Tzfat with its winding cobblestone streets and eclectic artist colonies, the stark desert landscape and hazy saltwater of the Dead Sea. I felt like I had relived key chapters of history by visiting these sites whose names are scattered throughout the pages of our Bibles.

My inclusion on a Birthright Israel trip was unlikely to begin with. Birthright Israel is an educational tourism organization whose mission, through partnering with the state of Israel and private philanthropists, "is to give every Jewish young adult around the world, especially the less connected, the opportunity to visit Israel on an educational trip."[1] At almost twenty-seven, I was barely making it in before the age cutoff, and I was by far the oldest participant on my particular trip; most were between eighteen and twenty-two.

In an era when Jews entering adulthood often drift away from their Jewish identity and heritage, the goal of the trip is to instill a deeper connection with Judaism through an encounter with the biblical and historical homeland of the Jewish people. Since the program was founded in 1999, over 750,000 participants representing sixty-eight countries have taken part in Birthright Israel trips. Oh, did I mention that Birthright trips are *free*?

As I increasingly came to identify as a Messianic Jew, I began to feel a deep stirring to visit Israel. The prominence of this land in the Bible and Jewish liturgy was becoming clear to me in a new way, and I felt strongly that understanding Israel was a key piece to understanding God's ongoing covenant with the Jewish people.

After hearing about a high school friend's experience on a Birthright trip, I had decided to apply. In my application, I was clumsy and upfront about my being a follower of Jesus and I was flatly denied a spot on the trip. Many Jews consider "conversion" to Christianity (a phrase I would never use to describe my own spiritual journey) to be an exit from Judaism, and there's certainly some truth to this conclusion. Historically, conversion language accurately reflects the reality that one was either Jewish or Christian (not both) and converting to Christianity offered the surest way to sever oneself from the ongoing life of the Jewish people. This was not how the first disciples of Jesus would have described themselves, and in our day, it is increasingly possible for faith in Jesus to lead one *deeper into* their Jewish identity as opposed to farther away from it.

I was disappointed that my application was rejected, and I laid the issue aside. But recently, I had been feeling a prompting to apply again. In fact, it became one of the few times in my life when I believe I heard directly—and clearly—from God. In the midst of praying about Birthright, I felt as though God literally interrupted my prayer and said, "I have already opened this door for you."

It was a strange experience, difficult to trust. I wasn't quite sure what to make of it, or if it had been real, but I took it as at least divine encouragement to listen to the impulse I'd been feeling. So I went through the process of applying again.

Wanting to get the full religious (and not merely cultural) experience of Israel, I applied with an Orthodox Jewish trip organizer. This time I was more discreet about my belief in Jesus, standing on the conviction that my purpose for going on the trip was not to evangelize, but merely to learn about and explore the land of my ancestors and the depth of my own Jewish identity. But I vowed to myself that I wouldn't hide it if the issue arose. I felt that I needed to be honest, which in my mind was not the same as volunteering unsolicited information.

My application seemed to sail through the bureaucratic powers that be, and it came down to the requisite interview with a rabbi that, I imagine, was typically a mere ten-minute formality. Not so in this case.

"Tell me, why are you interested in traveling to Israel?" asked Rabbi Stein, a representative of the group organizing the trip and my interviewer. I thought it was odd that he was calling at 5:00 p.m. in California (8:00 p.m. his time in New York), and he soon commented that he was way behind on finalizing details for this particular Birthright trip.

Mouth suddenly dry, I unexpectedly felt compelled to tell my story. I explained how becoming a follower of Jesus (I intentionally did not use the term "Christian") had spurred in me a deep desire to press into my Jewish identity. The rabbi listened intently, asking follow-up questions, and to my surprise the interview lasted an hour and a half. Most of that time was filled with lively conversation, and great interest on his part. Then he asked me a question that was met with silence on my end: "So, Jen, what have you found in Christianity that you didn't find in Judaism?"

As I pondered his question, there wasn't a quick and easy answer that came to mind. Messiah's atonement? Judaism has mechanisms for atonement as well. A sense of orientation for questions of faith? Judaism had been offering this long before Jesus ever came on the scene. Connection with God? Judaism's very essence was built upon this. "I'm not sure how to answer that question, rabbi," I finally responded, after a long pause in our conversation.

With that, the rabbi proceeded to tell me a bit of his own story. He had been raised with a Jewish mother and a Catholic father and had eventually come to a decision point about which tradition he would embrace as his own. He chose Judaism and had been pressing into the riches of Jewish life ever since.

Perhaps because of his own journey, Rabbi Stein permitted me to go on the trip. "Just don't make any waves," he cautioned, asking me not to speak about my faith in Jesus to anyone while on the trip. "And, though I won't be leading your trip, I'll be in Israel at the same time. I want to meet up with you in person to continue our conversation when we're both there."

Lech lecha. "Go from your country, your people and your father's household to the land I will show you" (Genesis 12:1). The command for Abraham to go to the land that God will reveal is embedded within the very basis of God's covenant with Abraham and his descendants. This intimate connection has endured throughout the centuries, and there has always been an unbreakable bond between the people of Israel and the land of Israel.

In the words of Rabbi Hayim Halevy Donin, the possession of the land of Israel functions as "the historical fulcrum of Israel's Covenant with God." He goes on to explain that

> It was only on the soil of Israel that all the commandments of the Lord could be implemented; it was only on the soil of Israel . . . that the permanent central sanctuary of the Jewish people could be built; it was only on the soil of Israel that the children of Israel would realize their fullest potential as a people; it was only on the soil of Israel that God's promises to Israel and His blessings would take on reality. . . . As the people were called upon to become a "holy people," their land was to be a "holy land."[2]

This reality is tightly woven into the corporate life and worship of the Jewish people. Three times a day, religious Jews recite the *Amidah*, or standing prayer, which (based on Isaiah 11:12) beseeches God to "raise high the banner to gather our exiles, and gather us together from the four quarters of the earth."[3]

After meals, Jews recite the *Birkat Hamazon*, in which we thank God for "having given as a heritage to our ancestors a precious, good and spacious land; for having brought us out, Lord our God, from the land of Egypt, and redeemed us from the house of bondage."[4]

The saddest day in the Jewish calendar is the Ninth of Av, on which Jews remember the destruction of Jerusalem by the Babylonians (in 586 BC) and the Romans (in AD 70). Both the annual Passover *seder* (traditional meal) and the liturgy for Yom Kippur, the Day of Atonement, conclude with the hopeful exhortation: "Next year in Jerusalem!"

Even during an extended exile from the land of Israel, the Jewish people did not stop hoping, praying, and believing that God would one day bring them back into their land. In one sense, times of exile have served to *strengthen* the bond between the Jewish people and the land of Israel. In the words of Jewish philosopher Franz Rosenzweig, the Jewish people are like "a knight truer to his land when he lingers in his travels and adventures and longs for the homeland it has left than in the times when he is at home."[5]

The enduring historical and theological connection between the land of Israel and the people of Israel is indisputable; the construct and narrative of the entire Old Testament is built upon the foundation of this connection, which has endured throughout the Jewish people's collective life ever since.

The question of the land becomes more complicated when Jesus and the emergence of Christianity are introduced. The function and importance of the land of Israel in the New Testament have proven to have a wide—and controversial—range of interpretation. Many conclude that the land of Israel loses its significance after the coming of Jesus, and the concept of a "holy land" is rendered obsolete.

Today, there is an additional layer of complexity that shrouds a biblical discussion of the land: the modern state of Israel. While the existence of the Jewish state is celebrated by the majority of Jews across the spectrum (a sentiment shared by many Christians), the deeply entrenched political situation threatens to cast its shadow over Christian perception of the land. Especially for New Testament scholars, to interpret Jesus as upholding God's covenantal promise of the land to the Jewish people runs the risk of implying some sort of tacit endorsement of the modern state and its politics.

And yet, the abiding centrality of the Promised Land endures throughout the New Testament and was central in the mission and message of Jesus.

꒰·꒱·꒱

As I packed for the trip, I carefully considered which books to bring and which to leave at home. I brought only a Tanakh (what Christians call the "Old Testament") and a few books—by Jewish authors—that I was working through for my doctoral dissertation. My only material connection to Jesus during the trip was my iPod, which was loaded with Christian worship music. I carefully excluded myself from the frequent "let's trade iPods!" game, which turned out to be a favorite activity among my fellow Birthright travelers on our many long bus rides.

As we toured the country, I would curl up in a window seat on the bus, worship music secretly playing in my ears, and gaze at the hills that led to the horizon. It struck me powerfully that this was the only place on earth that God ever beheld through human eyes and strode with human feet. It was the dust of this land that clung to his clothes and skin, and it was in these hills and valleys that he taught the parables we read in the Gospels. Upon first laying eyes on the shores of Tel Aviv after our long flight from New York, emotion welled up inside me as the tangible reality of the Jewish people's long exile, now finally over, stood before me.

We had spent our final Shabbat in Tzfat, and I woke up early on Saturday morning, pulled on a thick wool sweater, and headed to a small promenade overlooking the forested mountains of northern Israel. My roommate and the rest of the Birthright group were still sleeping, and I breathed in the crisp air, enjoying the quiet stillness that surrounded me. I opened my Tanakh to Isaiah and began reading in chapter 49. "Can a woman forget her nursing baby or lack compassion for a child of her womb? Even if these forget, I will not forget you. Behold, I have engraved you on the palms of My hands. Your walls are continually before Me" (Isaiah 49:15-16).

Looking out over the valley below, I marveled at God's commitment to the people of Israel, which included God's commitment to this particular plot of land. This people group engraved on God's hands, this place's walls ever before God's eyes. I was captivated by mystery and beauty, and on the final day of the trip I felt a sense of both fullness and yearning as I thought back over a very full ten days.

"Hello, Jen?" Rabbi Stein's words startled me out of my daydreaming. "It's good to finally meet you. How's your trip been?" He seated himself in the empty leather chair across from me, nudging it a little closer to mine.

"So nice to meet you as well, Rabbi Stein. The trip has been incredible. Thank you again for allowing me to be a part of it."

Amid the hustle and bustle of the busy hotel lobby, we continued the conversation we had begun two months earlier during the phone interview. He seemed genuinely curious to hear about my experience of Israel, and how it played into my unfolding faith journey.

"In light of these ten days spent in Israel, I think I finally have an answer to your question about what I've found in Christianity that I didn't find in Judaism," I told the rabbi.

His eyes widened a bit. "Oh, yeah? Please, go on."

I described to him an event that struck me on one of our touring days in Jerusalem, as our bus wound along Sultan Suleiman Street on the northern edge of the Old City, weaving in between the Damascus Gate and the Arab neighborhood of Bab a-Zahara. As we gazed out the windows at the Arabic writing on the buildings and hijab-wearing pedestrians, a collective attitude of fear and antipathy flowed through the bus. "I would never go into East Jerusalem," one of my fellow travelers remarked. "Me neither," chimed in another. "I could just never feel safe being surrounded by Arabs," concluded a third.

Indeed, the tensions between Jews and Arabs in the land are palpable and deep-seated. At times, there is a sense of hatred and rivalry that bubbles over into violence and retribution. "But," I mused to Rabbi Stein, "Jesus commands us to *love our enemies*. It's as if he absorbs hate rather than perpetuating it. And, somehow, I think we're supposed to do the same."

Rabbi Stein leaned back in his chair, pensive. "You're right," he replied after a long pause. "That is not a Jewish virtue."

ᔕᔕ•ᔕ•ᔕ

Many New Testament interpreters have attempted, in various ways, to downplay or eliminate the significance of the land. A meaningful connection to the land is viewed as an outdated and provincial dimension of Jewish religion that Jesus intentionally overcomes. These scholars write about a "spiritual" kingdom, within which there is no place for attachment to a particular piece of land. In short, they present a Jesus who showed no interest in the land of Israel and thus sharply diverged with the Judaism of his day on this point.

What is odd is that contemporary Christian scholarship and New Testament interpretation is increasingly focused on *reclaiming* the Jewishness of Jesus and the Jewishness of the text. However, this same body of scholarship reflects a deep skepticism toward any ongoing significance of the land, for Jesus and for Christians throughout the centuries.[6]

This leaves us with a profound inconsistency. To use an outdated analogy, it's like Mr. Jesus Potato Head. We adorn him with the things that seem noble and pure according to our modern, dignified standards and we leave off the things that seem odd, foreign, or difficult to explain. In the end, we have constructed Jesus in our own image, projecting our worldview backward onto him and his worldview. Because we aren't sure what do to with the centrality of the land throughout the Bible, or what it might mean for contemporary Christianity, we find rationale for simply doing away with it.

Not surprisingly, the complexity of modern Israeli politics tends to lie in the background of these "wardrobe" decisions; for some Christians, affirming Jesus' own connection to the land might unwittingly endorse the actions of the state of Israel, which is a controversial allegiance to have. There are Christians all along the political spectrum in this regard, spanning from those who fervently support the modern state of Israel and sanction its every action to those who champion the BDS movement[7] and the plight of the Palestinians (and other marginalized people groups in the Israeli political landscape). We must be careful *not* to read the political situation of our day back into a first-century context.

Thankfully, there is another emerging thread of Christian (and Messianic Jewish) scholarship, according to which we are missing something fundamental if we overlook the significance of the land in the New Testament. For example, in *The New Christian Zionism*,[8] we are introduced to a set of New Testament scholars and theologians who detect a vibrant, swirling current of land theology beneath the surface of a seeming dearth of land references in the New Testament.

Matthew scholar Joel Willitts argues that the Gospel's central focus on the "identity and significance of Jesus of Nazareth as Israel's long-awaited Messiah"[9] goes hand in hand with territorial restoration; in other words, Matthew takes this aspect of Jesus' kingdom proclamation for granted. It is *assumed*. In Willitts's words, "The restoration of Eretz Israel [the land of Israel] is a fundamental *presumption* of the chief theological implications of Matthew's story of Jesus."[10] The gospel expresses "an *abiding land consciousness* in line with the traditional Jewish territorial hope."[11]

This is yet another place where the issue of biblical translation rears its biased head. Those who believe that Jesus was not especially concerned with the little land of Israel but rather with the whole big world often cite Matthew 5:5: "Blessed are the meek, for they shall inherit the *earth*" (TLV italics added). And yet, there is a growing consensus among biblical scholars that this verse is actually better translated, "Blessed are the meek, for they shall inherit the *land*," as in the *land* of Israel.[12] This verse is no doubt echoing Psalm 37:11 ("But the meek will inherit the land and enjoy peace and prosperity"), where it is universally recognized that the Hebrew word *erets* refers to the land of Israel. In fact, the entirety of Psalm 37 expresses the reality that the land was always part of God's enduring covenant with the people of Israel (see, for example, Deuteronomy 30).

Mark Kinzer argues that the priority of the Promised Land is woven throughout the entire New Testament. In his work on Luke–Acts, he claims that the "Acts of the Apostles (read in light of the Gospel of Luke) presents an *euangelion* [gospel] that is directed especially to the Jewish people, and whose content relates to the consummation of Jewish history. That consummation involves the exile and return of the Jewish people to its land and its capital city."[13] Indeed, if we miss the ongoing significance of the *land* of Israel, we are missing a key component of God's enduring covenant with the *people* of Israel. Similarly, if we miss Jesus' own connection to and hope for the land, we are missing an integral part of his identity as Israel's Messiah.

꙰ • ꙰ • ꙰

What's ultimately at stake in a Christian affirmation of the ongoing theological significance of the land of Israel? First, to argue that the land no longer matters to Jesus and his followers is to drive a wedge between the New Testament and the Old Testament. Unfortunately, this wedge is all too prevalent in Christian biblical interpretation. To say that Jesus somehow undoes the centrality of the land in God's covenant with Israel likewise positions Jesus in juxtaposition to the Jewish people. In short, if we are to properly understand the gospel, we must understand what the land meant to Jesus in his proclamation of God's coming kingdom.

This common juxtaposition brings us to a second point. To overlook or deny the ongoing significance of the land reveals a failure to understand and accurately represent Judaism. The land has always been embedded within the Jewish people's covenantal identity and relationship with God, a connection that goes back to the call of Abraham in Genesis 12 and continues right up to today. In fact, we are living in a remarkable era in which the Jewish people are once again sovereign in their land, for the first time in two thousand years.

While Judaism's relationship to the land is layered and multi-faceted, and while the issue of modern Israeli politics looms large, it is an undeniable fact that the land of Israel is a central component of God's election of the Jewish people. If our goal is to understand Judaism, we cannot brush this important fact under the rug. Accordingly, if we want to understand Jesus the Jew, we must press into this aspect of Jesus' identity and orientation to the world.

In the end, a Christian affirmation of the ongoing significance of the land of Israel is part and parcel of a Christian commitment to solidarity with the Jewish people. If the people of Israel and the body of Messiah are joined together as the one people of God, then the concerns of the Jewish community ought to also be the concerns of the Christian church.

Currently, we are seeing a rise in global anti-Semitism as well as a resurgence of extreme stances against the state of Israel and its legitimacy. The *new anti-Semitism* is a term used to describe an extreme anti-Zionist[14] position that condemns the state of Israel and is increasingly fueling virulent forms of hatred toward the Jewish people.

The Israeli and wider Middle Eastern political landscape is undeniably and irreducibly complicated. At the same time, Israel is all too often scapegoated for the region's ongoing tensions, with the media tending to ignore Israel's unparalleled efforts at preserving the welfare of its own citizens as well as the welfare of those positioned as Israel's enemies. While Christians need not endorse every action of Israel's government, a certain fluency regarding key issues and a commitment to advocacy for the Jewish people worldwide demonstrates a concrete commitment to the well-being of God's covenant people, the root onto which the Christian church has been grafted.

6

BODIES

*To withhold our bodies from religion
is to exclude religion from our lives.*

DALLAS WILLARD

"Jen, can you dim the lights?"

I was with a group of Messianic Jewish friends, some of whom were gradually becoming my primary spiritual community. We had spent Shabbat afternoon together, laughing, eating, and sharing stories. There's something magical about Shabbat in Judaism, and this particular Shabbat was no exception. I felt increasingly *myself* the more I embraced my Jewish identity, and this community of Messianic Jews was helping me to live into the connection between my Jewishness and my faith in Messiah.

Now, the sun had set and three stars had appeared in the sky, the telltale indicator that Shabbat was over and it was the beginning of a new week. I dimmed the lights, and my friend Joshua lit the braided candle and began to sing the melody of the Havdalah liturgy. The word *havdalah* in Hebrew means separation, and this short little service marks the end of Shabbat on Saturday evening.

HAVDALAH LITURGY

Behold, God is my salvation. I will trust and not be afraid.
(Isaiah 12)

The Lord, the Lord, is my strength and my song.

He has become my salvation.

With joy you will draw water from the springs of salvation.

Salvation is the Lord's; on Your people is Your blessing, Selah.
(Psalm 3)

The Lord of hosts is with us,

the God of Jacob is our stronghold, Selah. (Psalm 46)

Lord of hosts: happy is the one who trusts in You. (Psalm 84)

Lord, save! May the King answer us on the day we call.
(Psalm 20)

For the Jews there was light and gladness,

joy and honor—so may it be for us. (Esther 8)

I will lift the cup of salvation and call on the name of the Lord.
(Psalm 116)

Blessed are You, Lord our God, King of the Universe,
who creates the fruit of the vine.

Blessed are You, Lord our God, King of the Universe,
who creates the various spices.

Blessed are You, Lord our God, King of the Universe,
who creates the lights of fire.

Blessed are You, Lord our God, King of the Universe,
who distinguishes between sacred and secular, between
light and darkness, between Israel and the nations, between
the seventh day and six days of work. Blessed are You, Lord,
who distinguishes between sacred and secular.

Havdalah is a particularly vivid illustration of the embodied nature of Jewish spirituality in that it powerfully engages all five senses. After some introductory prayers (composed of verses drawn from the Psalms, Isaiah, and Esther), we bless a cup of wine. *Blessed are You, Lord our God, King of the Universe, who creates the fruit of the vine.*

The significance of wine (and bread) in Judaism is the precursor to Jesus' institution of the Lord's Supper, and this is one of the many times wine is used for ceremonial purposes. Shabbat is ushered in with a cup of wine on Friday night and Shabbat goes out with the wine of Havdalah, reminding us of the sweetness of Shabbat and God's enduring presence with us even when Shabbat ends.

Then, we say a blessing over a small jar of spices, usually sweet-smelling spices like cinnamon and cloves, and everyone present smells them. *Blessed are You, Lord our God, King of the Universe, who creates various spices.*

While there are many different interpretations of the significance of the spices (two Jews, three opinions, remember?), my favorite is that they revive us from the sadness of Shabbat ending. This is an important window into how Jews experience Shabbat, and Torah more generally. While from the outside Jewish observance may look like a bunch of dusty and restricting rules, the truth is that Jews generally *delight* in the Torah. Psalm 119 offers a wonderful portrait of this concept. For example, verse 35: "Direct me in the path of your commands, for there I find delight" and verse 72, "The law from your mouth is more precious to me than thousands of pieces of silver and gold."

This is especially true for Shabbat. It's a time to step away from the pressures of the workday world and embrace the joy and beauty of family and fellowship. That observant Jews also disengage from technology on Shabbat is especially powerful, countercultural, and liberating.

Next, we say a blessing over the light of the braided Havdalah candle. *Blessed are You, Lord our God, King of the Universe, who creates the lights of fire.*

Like wine, candlelight is rife with significance in Judaism, as it is in Christianity. Shabbat is ushered in with lighting candles and lighting the Havdalah candle marks the end of Shabbat, as the Torah prohibits kindling a fire *on* Shabbat (Exodus 35:3). That Jesus comes as the light of the world (and commissions his followers to be the same) infuses new meaning and significance into Jewish traditions like Havdalah and the celebration of Hanukkah.

As we say this blessing, we hold our hands up to the fire and reflect on their translucence, yet another reminder that it is through our bodies that we experience and know God. Finally, the Havdalah liturgy concludes with a litany of distinctions, reminding us that the very foundation of creation is built upon distinctions.

So, in a mere five-minute Havdalah ceremony, we have *tasted* the wine, *smelled* the spices, *looked* upon the flame, *heard* the melodious songs, and *touched* the spice jar. Havdalah offers one small glimpse into Judaism's thoroughly embodied spirituality.

∽·∽·∽

Around 370 BC, the illustrious Greek philosopher Plato wrote the dialogue *Phaedrus*. Here Plato lays out his famous chariot allegory to explain his view of the human soul. According to the analogy, the soul is like a pair of winged horses with their charioteer. One of the horses is white and represents all that is noble and praiseworthy, while the other horse is black and represents the opposite. If a soul is unable to harness the black horse, it loses its wings, is pulled down to earth and incarnated in a body. This is Plato's version of a kind of "fall," an account of cosmic catastrophe that leaves the world in its current state. Notably, for Plato, the fact that we have bodies is the result of something *having gone terribly wrong*.

This account fits into Plato's larger philosophy of dualism. For dualists, there are essentially two separate worlds, one which is physical, material, and temporal, and the other which is invisible, ethereal, and eternal. As we see in the chariot allegory, our bodies belong to the material world and are thus chained to the physical processes of change, decline, and ultimately death. Our souls, however, originate in the unseen spirit world and after death return to it for reward or punishment.[1]

According to this paradigm, the goal of spirituality is to somehow transcend our bodies and the physical world in order to attain a higher, disembodied plane of existence. Our bodies are thus the primary obstacle to the spiritual life; if we can figure out how to restrain and control them, we are on the way to finally leaving them behind.

Does any of this sound familiar to you? Does it sound biblical? The fascinating reality is that the New Testament was penned in a Greco-Roman environment, where these ideas carried the day. And yet, this worldview is sharply distinct from a Jewish, Hebraic worldview. While these two versions of reality seem to war against each other in certain New Testament passages (see, for example, Romans 7:21-24 and Colossians 3:1-5), after the parting of the ways, the Greco-Roman version ends up dominating the Christian narrative (particularly Protestant, evangelical theology) while the Jewish-Hebraic version dominates the Jewish narrative, with very few historical exceptions.

As Jewish historian of religion Daniel Boyarin explains, Christianity has generally conceived of human beings as *embodied souls*, while Judaism has conceived of human beings as *ensouled bodies*.[2] When I teach on this concept, I write these two definitions of humanity on the whiteboard and ask my students to analyze and contrast them. While some students prematurely remark that they are essentially saying the same thing, what we unpack together is that each definition is formed by combining a noun and an adjective.

According to the classic Christian understanding, we are primarily souls that are housed in bodies. Even the phrase *embodied souls* connotes the image of our souls being somehow stuck or trapped in our bodies, like they would be better off untethered and disembodied. The phrase implies, at the very least, that a disembodied soul is *possible*.[3]

According to the Jewish understanding, we are primarily bodies. Bodies that, to be sure, have a soul, which suggests that there can also be bodies without souls (such as animals, perhaps?). In any case, if we are *ensouled bodies*, then having a body is fundamentally what it means to be human.

Do you see the difference? When we think about what it means to be human, the way we constitute humanity matters profoundly. If we think our bodies are an accidental and unfortunate part of our being human, we will approach them from a particular disposition. Likewise, believing that they are a constitutive part of what makes us who we are will cause us to act a certain way toward them.

かか・かか・かか

In college, I first began seriously investigating the claims of Christianity and engaging in Christian community in the context of a Vineyard church plant in San Luis Obispo, CA. There's a story about John Wimber, the founder of the Vineyard church movement, that significantly informed the identity of this particular Vineyard congregation.

As the story goes, John Wimber became a Christian by reading the Gospels, and then approached the pastor of the church he was attending. "When do we get to *do the stuff*?" he asked. "Eh, what stuff?" the pastor replied. "You know, the stuff Jesus does in the Gospels. Healing the sick, casting out demons, raising the dead." The pastor looked at him, dumbfounded. "Um, we don't actually *do* those things . . . we just believe that Jesus did them."

And so Wimber went on to found the Vineyard and "do the stuff." This is the context in which I became a follower of Messiah, and so my own faith was colored not only by "doing the stuff," but by the necessarily embodied vision for human life and flourishing that this model of ministry entails. In the church where I was first exposed to Christianity, there was no real separation between spiritual life and physical life; the two were seen as completely intertwined and mutually informing.

Just like with my experience at St. John's Episcopal Church in New Haven, it is only in looking back that I see how Jewish this particular impulse is. Judaism is a religion that has always been carried out through engaging the body; attempting to escape bodily reality would be to miss the richness of faith and its enactment. And so, my becoming a follower of Jesus in a Vineyard church makes all the sense in the world—it was yet another way that God was allowing my Jewish identity to find expression in my newfound faith in Christ.

The summer before my senior year in college, I read Dallas Willard's book *The Spirit of the Disciplines: Understanding How God Changes Lives* with a group of Christians who were deeply invested in this particular Vineyard church. The role of our bodies in the spiritual life is the jumping off point for Willard's writing, and this book has been one of the most significant influences on my spiritual journey ever since.

Willard indicts the contemporary church for its relative insig-
nificance, naming deep-seated dualism as the cause. He writes, "If
salvation is to affect our lives, it can do so only by affecting our
bodies. If we are to participate in the reign of God, it can only be
by our actions. And our actions are physical—we live only in the
processes of our bodies. *To withhold our bodies from religion is to
exclude religion from our lives*."[4]

◡•◡•◡

As we saw with Havdalah, Judaism has much to teach us about
embodiment and what it looks like to engage our bodies in worship
and discipleship. In fact, it has much to teach us about how to read
the New Testament. Let's take the Lord's Prayer, for example. For
some, the words are so familiar that we can easily bypass the
process of actually entering into and meditating on their meaning:
"Your kingdom come, your will be done, on earth as it is in heaven"
(Matthew 6:10).

Did you catch that? It does not say "swoop us up to heaven, so
that we can be in the place where your will is done." The imagery is
of the downward movement of God's kingdom, its presence and
reality breaking into *this world*, not of us transcending this physical,
material world. This world is where God's kingdom is coming, and
we are commissioned to be ambassadors of that kingdom—here
and now, in these bodies. This is not platonic dualism.

I sometimes wonder if Jews understand the notion of God's
coming kingdom better than many Christians. Judaism is not a
religion where lots of time is spent contemplating the afterlife, or
what will happen when we die. It's a religion that is lived out here
and now, in the world and in the body. This is actually what the
Torah is all about; it provides concrete instructions for how to live
holy lives, and these instructions are *quite bodily*. They have to do

with genital discharges and skin diseases, what we eat and what we wear. They teach us how to order our lives, which necessarily means what we do with our bodies.

In a profound way, the Torah for Jews offers a remarkable parallel to the spiritual disciplines of the Christian life, as described by Willard. Both teach us how to live in the world, how to orient ourselves toward the kingdom, and how to live faithfully in the midst of real life. Both remind us that spirituality is not primarily what happens when we die, but rather about how we live.

Herein lies a key connection to what we discussed in the previous chapter. A "landed" gospel has everything to do with an "embodied" kingdom. God formed the first human being, Adam, out of the earth (Hebrew, *adamah*), tipping us off to this connection from the very beginning. In case we think this is an outdated Old Testament thing, the incarnation of God in Jesus is perhaps the most poignant illustration of God's enduring concern for this physical, material world.

God immerses Godself in the created order, which says a lot about what our vocation as Christ followers should look like. Given the centrality of the incarnation in the Christian story, it's fascinating to me that so often our goal essentially becomes *ex-carnation*, or freedom from our bodies. Odd, isn't it?

A closer look reveals that the related themes of land and bodies are a *continual thread throughout the entire story of the Bible*. We see it in the Genesis creation narrative, we see it in Israel the people's connection to Israel the land, we see it powerfully in the incarnation, and we see it in the glimpses we get of where all of this is heading. In the biblical portraits of the end of the age, what we see is a *garden* in the midst of a *city* (see, for example, Revelation 22:1-5 and Isaiah 11:6-16).

The Bible does not point forward to disembodied spirits floating around in some airy place called heaven; it points toward *new creation*, a redeemed and restored version of the material world where every tear is wiped away from every eye and there is no longer death or mourning or crying or pain (Revelation 21:4).[5]

After all, as Paul reminds us in 1 Corinthians 15, the entire Christian faith hangs on the bodily resurrection of Jesus. Even after he is raised from the dead, Jesus still has a body. Um, hello, does it seem like the Bible might care about bodies?! As Willard makes clear, the challenge of embodiment—and the means we often employ to avoid it—is a pressing (if often unrecognized) issue for the Christian church.

$\backsim\cdot\backsim\cdot\backsim$

While all of this ought to serve as an empowering and intriguing reminder of the grandeur of embodied existence, it is also, in some ways, excruciating. I remember a phone call that I had with Samantha, a student of mine, who was processing through these concepts as I taught them in her Christian theology class. "If all of this is true," she said slowly, "then death and disease are a lot worse than I thought."

She went on to explain how she had been raised in a Christian culture where funerals were essentially celebrations, for the deceased was now happily "in a better place." For her, this type of Christian spirituality had taken away the sting of death, and in turn short-circuited the process of grief and mourning that death provokes.

Samantha's experience with physical challenges was similar. She had been diagnosed with cancer several years before, and she had been both encouraged and bewildered by her Christian community's response. Their chorus to her was all about the temporariness of her body, and how she would one day be free from it. The desire was to encourage her, though it had ended up alienating her. And so, when she had encountered these ideas in my class, the implications were freighted with uncertainty.

She and I went on to have a profound and weighty conversation about the gospels, and about how Jesus doesn't hover around, three feet off the ground. He doesn't remain distant from the real life (and real body) struggles of those around him. He doesn't encourage those suffering to just hang on until death brings them into glory, and he doesn't rejoice when someone dies.

Physical healing and restoration undergird the kingdom that Jesus brings. Jesus had compassion on the woman with the problem of bleeding, and he healed her. In John 11, even though he was just about to raise Lazarus from the dead, *Jesus wept*. He wept alongside Mary and Martha in their anguish. He recognized that, even in the face of God incarnate, death is the enemy. Death is the reminder that we still live in a broken world. To minimize death or the mourning that comes with it is to cheapen not only the human experience, but the biblical witness itself.

Once again, Judaism has much to teach us in this regard. In Jewish practice, mourning is a formal ritual. After the burial of an immediate family member, the bereaved enter into a seven-day period called *shiva*. In classic Jewish fashion, there is a long list of what can and cannot be done during this interval. One tears their clothes (a practice we see throughout the Bible), generally does not leave their house, and sits either on the floor or on a low stool. Shiva is followed by a less intensive thirty days of mourning, and the entire year following the loved one's death, one is still in a state of mourning.

Part of what mourning in Judaism entails is reciting a traditional Jewish prayer called the Mourner's Kaddish. Lest we think that Jews are drawn into the depths of despair because they recognize death as the enemy, the Mourner's Kaddish is simply and straightforwardly a declaration of God's greatness and worthiness of praise, and a beckoning for God's kingdom to come and to bring with it great and lasting peace. The very real sting of death sits side by side with a blunt acknowledgment of God's sovereignty and goodness. Judaism as a whole is much more comfortable embracing the profound tensions that Christian theology all too fervently seeks to resolve.

MOURNER'S KADDISH

Glorified and sanctified be God's great name
throughout the world
which He has created according to His will.
May He establish His kingdom in your lifetime
and during your days,
and within the life of the entire House of Israel, speedily and soon;
and say, Amen.
May His great name be blessed forever and to all eternity.
Blessed and praised, glorified and exalted, extolled and honored,
adored and lauded be the name of the Holy One, blessed be He,
beyond all the blessings and hymns, praises and consolations that
are ever spoken in the world; and say, Amen.
May there be abundant peace from heaven, and life, for us
and for all Israel; and say, Amen.
He who creates peace in His celestial heights,
may He create peace for us and for all Israel;
and say, Amen.

Notably, there must be a minyan for one to recite the Mourner's Kaddish. Judaism recognizes that mourning is a complex process and that it must be done in the midst of community. It is the community's responsibility to gather around the bereaved, for it is their presence that allows the mourner to recognize and name God's presence in the midst of grief and loss.

Without acknowledging the gravity of death, we cannot fully appreciate the victory that Christ has brought in conquering it. In short, we cannot fully comprehend the gospel. The gospel of Jesus is not a "get out of hell free" card, nor is it the guarantee that we will one day float around in a faraway place called heaven.

The gospel of Jesus is about God's kingdom and its power and presence in and among us. It is about God's final and definitive "no" to all of the forces that work against human life and flourishing. For us, it is about living into this kingdom, shaping our lives around it, and pointing others toward it. In short, it is about the outward expansion of holiness that Jesus embodied.

If it is to be these things, the Christian life cannot hover above the material world, just hanging on until we get to go to a better place. On the flip side, the lives we live now are not just polishing the china on the Titanic. The end is not disembodied souls in heaven, but embodied life in God's *new creation*. God is in the business of making all things new, not trashing this world and drawing wraithlike souls up to heaven. "Your kingdom come, your will be done, on earth as it is in heaven." This is the prayer that Jesus taught his disciples to pray, and this is the work that discipleship entails.

To be ambassadors of *this* kingdom means to care deeply about bodies and the forces of death that oppose them. It is about engaging the real-life issues that bombard us, issues like racial inequality and political corruption and grieving neighbors and the lives of the unborn. If God is working to redeem this world, our view of who is "serving the kingdom"—and what this looks like—needs to expand.

While we may not be able to repair all of the brokenness that surrounds us, this reality cannot be an excuse for not working toward redemption in our little corner of the world and in our circles of influence. In the words of Rabbi Tarfon, who lived a generation after Jesus, "It is not your duty to finish the work, but neither are you at liberty to neglect it."[6]

The classic "starfish story" offers a wonderful illustration of this idea. According to the story, an old man was walking on the beach at dawn when he noticed a small girl picking up starfish stranded by the retreating tide and throwing them back into the sea one by one. He went up to her and asked her why she was doing this. The young girl replied that the starfish would die if left exposed to the morning sun. "But the beach goes on for miles, and there are thousands of starfish. You will not be able to save them all. How can your effort make a difference?" The girl looked at the starfish in her hand and then threw it to safety in the waves. "To this one, it makes a difference."[7]

7

SIN AND THE FALL

So I live with the conflict. I live with it every day,
in a thousand ways that pull me in one direction or another.
I have come to realize that the conflict is a sign of my health,
not of my confusion; the tension is a measure of the richness
of my life, not of its disorderliness.

BLU GREENBERG

It was early evening in Helsinki, almost dusk, and the narrow path curved along the wooded retreat grounds, tall trees casting their long shadows over the underbrush around us. I was walking with Richard Harvey, another Messianic Jewish scholar, whom I had met at a conference a few months prior and I was deeply grateful for the opportunity to spend more time with him.

As we walked, he was encouraging me to continue to press forward with my dissertation. I had been stalled out for a number of months, lost in the research and its all-too-tight connection to my own layered identity. I felt ashamed about the lack of progress I was making, and I appreciated Richard's ability to understand the complexity of it all.

"It's important work that you're doing, Jen. Not just for your own sake, but for all of us," Richard exhorted. As it would turn out, that conversation was a sort of turning point, as was my time in Helsinki in general.

It was the summer of 2010, and I had been invited there for what would become the inaugural meeting of the Helsinki Consultation on Jewish Continuity in the Body of Messiah, an international gathering of Jewish followers of Jesus from all across the ecclesial spectrum. There were three Catholic priests, four Eastern Orthodox Christians, one Lutheran, and five Messianic Jews. We hailed from eight different countries, all of us seeking to negotiate our Jewishness and our faith in Christ from the very different communities and contexts in which we had landed.

Over the next ten years, this group would become a mainstay in my spiritual life. We would meet in a different European city every summer, and it was an event I looked forward to the entire year. There was a unique and indescribable bond between us, as we shared a set of fundamental commonalities that undergird our very different lives and communities and theologies. We felt connected, across the miles and amid our radically divergent liturgical lives. Each year we held a public conference centered around a particular theme, and each year we drafted a statement about our time together and the agreement we had struggled to reach.[1]

And yet, a sense of deep difference has endured, continually revealing the fragility of our fellowship. Ironically, two of the Catholics (one a Dominican priest and the other a Jesuit priest) would argue intensely over just about everything, which eventually became a running joke among the group. "Here they go again," we would all laugh.

It wasn't all just joking, though. The Jesuit priest, Fr. David, repeatedly felt as though he was holding the group back, that maybe we would be better off without him. At certain moments, our views were so different that what held us together became blurred, even seemingly obscured.

For me, the diversity of the group is exactly what has always constituted its richness. It is precisely the difference in our viewpoints, all trying to make sense of the same truths and realities, that makes our group so dynamic and so drawn to one another. Each year we would host the public conference during the day and continue the (often heated) discussions long into the nights. And each year, miraculously, we would feel our collective bond growing even deeper.

The dynamism-amid-toil that I experienced in this group was a large part of what energized me to finish my dissertation, which focused on key twentieth- and twenty-first-century developments in Jewish-Christian relations and the changing nature of the very relationship between the two religious traditions.[2] I increasingly saw and experienced that, rather than being a force for division, diversity and difference can actually create a new sense of cohesion and coherence.

☙ · ☙ · ☙

Judaism and Christianity develop in divergent directions in the aftermath of the parting of the ways, and the profound differences between each religious tradition can be entered into and observed through any number of portals and perspectives. As I was working on my dissertation, one divergence in particular became a central focus, both in my research and in my own theological wrestling. Amid the deep gaps between Judaism and Christianity lies a different understanding of human sin and the so-called fall. This is one of the doctrinal divisions I have struggled with the most, striving to find a way forward in my teaching and writing.[3]

According to the classic Reformed Christian paradigm, there are essentially four acts in the unfolding divine drama that Scripture tells of and that we continue to live out. First, *creation*, which is often considered to have existed in some sort of perfection according to the Christian tradition.

Quickly, however, comes *the fall*, the point at which humanity turns away from God and the creation project is set off kilter. Sin enters the world and the entire created order becomes tainted and tarnished. Many Christians read the Old Testament as an extended commentary on the fall; the "law" was an attempt to restrain human sinfulness that failed because it only addressed externals, never dealing with human waywardness in its deepest forms.

The next chapter of the story, *redemption*, begins when Christ comes into the darkness of fallen creation, rescuing humanity from its hopeless and helpless baseness. Finally, the entire drama points toward *new creation*, of which we get glimpses in certain prophetic passages and the book of Revelation.

Does this paradigm sound familiar to you? Have you heard it described in sermons? You may be nodding your head along in agreement as you read about these four acts. They may put language to a concept you've heard over the years. Even outside Reformed Christian circles, this well-trod narrative has shaped the way Christians have read their Bibles and preached the gospel for centuries.

However, as I wrestled with the ongoing vocation of the people of Israel in my doctoral studies, I increasingly saw that this model has no room for such a notion. Despite clearly being the subject of our Old Testament (two-thirds of the Christian Bible!), Israel gets either left out of the story entirely or construed as an extended example of human sinfulness and ineffectuality. Was this truly the full extent of Israel's purpose in the plan of God? Did Israel's role really end with the coming of Jesus the Redeemer?

I began to press into the dominant narrative that grounds Jewish biblical interpretation and self-understanding, and I was surprised to realize how very different it is from this familiar Christian structuring of the story. While Judaism's doctrine of creation is generally quite similar to Christianity's, the real divergence begins with Genesis 3.

Both traditions affirm the fundamental goodness of creation, humanity being created in the image of God, and the covenant between God and humanity creating a kind of joint venture going forward. For both traditions, the Genesis creation narrative counteracts dualism, as the physical, material world is repeatedly deemed good precisely in its substance and materiality. Ultimately, however, a robust Christian endorsement of physicality is short-lived.

While Christian tradition tends to attribute a kind of perfection to creation, Jewish tradition sees it as *good* but not yet *holy*. Holiness is instituted with the Sabbath in Genesis 2 and finds fuller expression in the book of Exodus through the people of Israel and their corporate life. This variance ends up being quite significant.

For much of Christian history (crystallized by Augustine in the fourth century), Genesis 3 has served as a pivot point in the narrative. In Adam's fall, all of humanity falls. A chasm is created between God and humanity, and the darkness of the fall casts its shadow backward onto the goodness of creation.

In the words of John Calvin, "As it was the spiritual life of Adam to remain united and bound to his Maker, so estrangement from him was the death of his soul. Nor is it any wonder that he consigned his race to ruin by his rebellion when he perverted the whole order of nature on heaven and on earth." Calvin goes on to explain that, on account of Adam's disobedience, "the heavenly image was obliterated in him" and that "he also entangled and immersed his offspring in the same miseries."[4]

This is a classic Christian description of the doctrine of "original sin," which construes Adam's sin as a kind of disease that his offspring are indelibly born with. The inheritance of this sinful state "does not rest upon imitation,"[5] is transmitted from one generation to the next, overturns the entire person, and corrupts all of creation. Herein lies the Christian (Reformed) doctrine of "total depravity." It's important to note that, in the thought of Calvin and others, the ultimate effect of such a strong and potent doctrine of original sin is to further magnify the work of Christ and its effects.

Most Christians are surprised to learn that Jews read Genesis 3 in an entirely different light. According to a Jewish reading of the text, Adam's sin does not predetermine the decisions of his offspring. In Judaism, humanity is understood to be endowed with a *yetzer hara* (evil inclination) and a *yetzer hatov* (good inclination) that dwell within each of us. The phrase "evil inclination" can even be a bit misleading; according to widespread Jewish understanding, the yetzer hara is not in and of itself bad. It is, rather, the part of a human being that draws one downward, toward concern for the more mundane aspects of life. According to one Jewish *midrash*, without the yetzer hara, a person would not build a house, get married, have children, etc.[6]

That being said, the yetzer hara is also that which can and often does lead us to commit sinful acts. As the element of humanity that draws us downward, it tempts human beings toward the gratification and advancement of self. This is precisely the problem that Adam's choices demonstrate so clearly. However, according to classic Jewish thought, *human obedience is possible*, unlike in Calvin's narration.

A key window into this Jewish framework is Deuteronomy 30, one of the "blessings and curses" passages where God promises to Israel life and prosperity should they obey and walk in his ways, and destruction and exile should they turn away and worship idols. Lest we believe this is some pie in the sky impossibility, Deuteronomy 30:11 assures the Israelites that "what I am commanding you today is not too difficult for you or beyond your reach." The element of true human free will remains alive and well in Jewish tradition, even after the so-called fall of Adam.

ᘓ·ᘓ·ᘓ

From our very first meeting, the Helsinki Consultation developed a shared vision to foster a global community of Jewish disciples of Jesus from all across the church and synagogue world. We dreamed (and debated!) about what this might look like each time we were together. Then, in 2018, this vision took its first step toward becoming a reality.

We invited a group of fifty Jewish believers in Jesus to join us in Dallas, Texas, on the campus of The King's University and Gateway Church, to partner in our long-held dream. In a remarkable way, this larger group experienced the same deep bond among significant differences that our smaller group had experienced in Helsinki and had been deepening ever since.

The term "existential loneliness" became like a hashtag for our time in Dallas; all of us felt isolated and alone in different ways, and finding one another was like finding a spring in the desert. We offered to each other a whole new group of kindred spirits, all of us facing many of the same struggles in our very different contexts.

In the aftermath of the Dallas meeting, the organization Yachad BeYeshua (Together in Jesus) was formed.[7] Its existence raises the question whether God might be working in a particular way within the Jewish segment of the body of Christ, and it hopefully raises one more banner that Jewish identity endures, even within that body.

As has always been the case with the Helsinki Consultation, the dynamism and intrigue of Yachad BeYeshua is built upon the depth of our differences and yet the commonality of our core identities. While we are all seeking to negotiate the two central pieces of our religious selves—our Jewishness and our faith in Messiah—some of us find the most authentic way to do so is through the Messianic Jewish movement. Others have found their spiritual home in the Catholic or Eastern Orthodox Church, while still others spiritually reside in historic Protestant or nondenominational churches.

And yet, for each and every one of us, our Jewishness *still means something*. It isn't erased in the waters of baptism. For Christian theologian Kendall Soulen, the church's ability to recognize the ongoing significance of Jewish identity—particularly within the church—is the litmus test of its ability to overcome supersessionist theology (which posits, in one way or another, that the church replaces Israel as the people of God). If the people of Israel are, in the end, more than an extended example of human sinfulness displayed throughout the Old Testament, the issue of Jewish identity within the church raises a pointed and pressing question.

What exactly Jewish identity means, and whether it lays any ongoing claim upon those who bear it, has been a lively discussion since the beginning of the Helsinki Consultation that continues on in Yachad BeYeshua. The range of perspectives within our fellowship is mirrored in a poignant way through the life of one particular Jewish follower of Jesus, whose life slightly predates the emergence of the Helsinki group, yet whose influence lives on. Aaron Jean-Marie Lustiger, the "Jewish Cardinal," was born in 1926 in Paris to Jewish Polish parents and went on to become a Catholic and serve as the archbishop of Paris and a cardinal in the Catholic Church.

While Lustiger is by no means the first Jew to enter the Christian church, both his prominence and his refusal to renounce his Jewish identity make his story significant. In his words, "In becoming a Christian, I did not intend to cease being the Jew I was then. I was not running away from the Jewish condition. I have that from my parents and I can never lose it. I have it from God and he will never let me lose it."[8]

Orthodox Jewish theologian Michael Wyschogrod wrote a letter to Cardinal Lustiger in which he raised a number of important issues. In the letter, Wyschogrod challenges Lustiger on what it means to claim Jewish identity, and what is at stake in how Lustiger appropriates that identity within the Catholic Church.[9] As he explained in the letter, "To be a Jew means to labor under the yoke of the commandments. . . . Once someone has come under the yoke of the commandments, there is no escaping this yoke. So baptism, from the Jewish point of view, does not make eating pork into a neutral act. In fact, nothing a Jew can do enables him to escape from the yoke of the commandments."[10]

For Wyschogrod, Lustiger's Jewish identity makes a demand upon him, as does the identity of every Jew by virtue of God's covenant with the Jewish people. Wyschogrod highlights this reality for Lustiger, whose refusal to disavow his Jewishness presented an opportunity to publicly refute the reality whereby becoming a Christian means ceasing to be a Jew.

"Throughout the centuries," Wyschogrod wrote to Lustiger, "Jews who entered the Church very quickly lost their Jewish identity. Within several generations they intermarried and the Jewish traces disappeared. . . . In short, if all Jews in past ages had followed the advice of the Church to become Christians, there would be no more Jews in the world today."

In light of this historical reality, Wyschogrod raises a key question: "Does the Church really want a world without Jews? Does the Church believe that such a world is in accordance with the will of God? Or does the Church believe that it is God's will, even after the coming of Jesus, that there be a Jewish people in the world?"[11]

This central question lies close to the heart of Yachad BeYeshua as an organization, and it is a question that is just making its way onto the radar screen of the wider Christian church.

ᴠᴨ·ᴠᴨ·ᴠᴨ

There is a more mystical branch of Judaism, within which exists an account of a cosmic catastrophe that is the closest thing Judaism has to a doctrine of the fall. Its contours, however, are quite different from Christianity's classic doctrine of sin.

In classic Christian theology, the central tension that drives the narrative forward in the aftermath of the "fall" is human sin and the need for salvation. While this *sin-salvation* paradigm characterizes a Christian understanding of the Bible, Judaism's central narrative is focused around creation's movement from being *good* to being *holy*. Rather than the hopeless plight of humanity being the driving force, Israel's vocation as the steward and locus of God's holiness moves the narrative forward. Within this *creation-consummation* paradigm, the goal is for all of creation to be blanketed with a knowledge of and orientation toward Israel's God.

There is a fascinating development that emerges within the Kabbalistic or mystical strand of Jewish thought, which is relevant to unpack here. While Jewish mysticism dates back to the Second Temple period, what interests us here is the emergence of Lurianic Kabbalah in the sixteenth century.

First, the context. As we have seen, the history between Judaism and Christianity is fraught with tension following the parting of the ways. The situation generally becomes even more complex and volatile once Islam comes onto the scene in the seventh century. However, amid the religious tensions that remain all too evident even in our day, history offered a remarkable (albeit temporary) reprieve in one particular era in one particular place.

Though the specific dates are debated, what is clear is that this "golden age" in southern Spain was characterized by peaceful coexistence and mutual influence between Jews, Christians, and Muslims.[12] Touring this region today offers a remarkable window into the depth and complexity of the reciprocal influencing that was at play during this incredible era.

While the fragile coexistence faced continual threats, it came definitively crashing down with the expulsion of the Jews from Spain in 1492 by the Catholic Monarchs, King Ferdinand II and Queen Isabella I. The trauma of this event was intense for the Jewish people, as the "golden age" had offered a kind of cultural flourishing that scarcely seemed possible in the enduring reality of exile from the land of Israel.

In the aftermath of the expulsion, some Jews from Spain made their way to Tzfat in northern Israel, which quickly became the geographical center of Jewish mysticism. One of these Jews was Isaac Luria. Having been influenced both by Christianity and the crumbling of an astounding era, Luria offered an explanation of cosmic catastrophe that may be the closest thing Judaism has to a doctrine of the fall.

Though the components are complex, the first basic movement (and remember, it's mysticism and thus not based on reason or logic) is *tzimtzum,* the notion that God must contract himself in order to make room for creation. God then infuses his presence back into his creation in the form of vessels of divine essence, but God's presence is too powerful for the vessels that contain it and they shatter.

This is the second movement, *shevirat ha-kelim* (breaking of the vessels), and the result is that fragments of divine presence are scattered and hidden throughout the created world. It becomes humanity's vocation (and in particular, the Jewish people's vocation) to gather and uncover the hidden fragments of divine light and presence. This is the third movement, *tikkun olam*, the concept of repairing a broken world, which has a long and rich history within Jewish tradition.

Mystical, far-fetched, and philosophical. I know. But what's fascinating is to analyze who is at fault and whose job it is to fix the problem. In the classic Christian narrative, the answers to these questions are quite clear. It is humanity's fault (by virtue of Adam's sin and our being his offspring) and it is God's job (through Christ) to fix the problem. In Lurianic Kabbalah (which, again, offers the closest thing Judaism has to a "fall" narrative), blame and commissioning are harder to dole out.

When I teach this concept to my Christian students, we always end up in a spirited discussion about these various issues. "Wait, so is Luria saying that the cosmic catastrophe is *God's* fault?!" one student asks, voice slightly elevated, incredulity evident. "No way," responds another, "it's not God's fault, it just *happens*. It's no one's fault!" What becomes clear is that it is *not* humanity's fault. Humanity is caught up in the mystical drama, and eventually commissioned to rebuild what has been lost.

"So human beings are responsible for redemption? That's impossible!" a third student insists. After we have sufficiently parsed the differences between the classic Christian narrative and the Lurianic

Kabbalistic narrative, we consider one final question: What can each narrative learn from the other?

What my students inevitably pinpoint is that the Jewish narrative takes human action seriously. To view human beings as hopelessly fallen and incapable of doing good (à la Calvin) can serve to diminish our God-given vocation in the world. Some of my students end up admitting that they have unwittingly viewed Christianity as a guarantee of eternal life, whereby life here and now matters little; it's just a time of waiting. In Judaism, humanity's vocation *matters*. Creation's movement from goodness to holiness depends on it.

Likewise, my students remark that the Jewish narrative doesn't take the reality of radical evil in our world seriously enough. What ails our existence is not just the scattering and hiddenness of God's presence; there is empirically something more malevolent than this. And so, redeeming evil must go beyond religious devotion and acts of kindness. We really do need a Savior, someone to redirect the whole trajectory in a way that humanity cannot do on its own.

Ultimately, the juxtaposition between the classic Christian narrative and Lurianic Kabbalah sheds new light on the incarnation. In Jesus, God inhabits creation as a participant within it. The incarnation is God's most scandalous act of engagement with creation, God's full self-revelation, *and* the means by which humankind can participate in the mending of the world. In Jesus, the God-man, we see both the fullness of divine redemption and the gravity of human vocation.

In the incarnation, God takes the initiative on humanity's behalf but in doing so does not bypass human action. Instead, God assumes our humanity in order to perfect creation and effect renewal and repair. In just this way, God invites all of humankind to become participants in this renewal, joining each small and local act of repair to God's single act of cosmic mending, like threads woven into a master tapestry.

What I love most about this discussion in my classes is that it challenges my Christian students to consider a narrative that is radically different from the one they find most familiar, and then to reevaluate their own grounding narrative in light of encountering another's. As I wrote about in my dissertation, this very process mirrors what has been happening between Jews and Christians in the years since the Holocaust. In stepping outside our own familiar terrain to explore different theological territory, we see new things upon returning to our framing narratives.

Fundamentally, this kind of substantive engagement across the boundary that separates Judaism and Christianity allows us to imagine what it might be like had history taken a different turn. What if there hadn't been a dramatic and final parting of the ways? What if each tradition hadn't come to define itself in mutual exclusion from the other?

These are the very same questions that Yachad BeYeshua raises, albeit from a different vantage point. Our substantial differences become a catalyst for new thinking and personal growth, which offers to us a remarkable lens through which to approach difference.

Holding onto Jewish identity while allowing faith in Jesus to find full expression is a bit like embracing the tension between the differing perspectives on sin and the fall we've just explored. Part of the challenge is renouncing the all-too-common assumption that difficulty and friction, tension and toil, indicate that something is wrong. Theologically speaking, what might it look like to *press into* tension, rather than seeking to resolve it? What might it mean to admit that the Bible's narrative includes diverse strands which resist being neatly categorized and systematized?

This may be yet another important theological contribution of the Messianic Jewish movement, whose in-between existence is by definition fraught with apparent incoherence. As Mark Kinzer once remarked to me, "I feel like my whole life has been spent trying to put together pieces that don't fit." Perhaps it is the very tensions that define our lives that paradoxically constitute the great richness of the human experience.

8

SABBATH

God completed—on the seventh day—
His work that He made, and He ceased—on the seventh day—
from all His work that He made.

GENESIS 2:2 TLV

Israel isn't that far from Croatia, is it?" my friend Amy asked, pulling up a map on her laptop. We were sitting on her couch, finalizing the itinerary for our grand summer adventure to celebrate her thirty-fifth birthday and my finishing my PhD. "Um, I don't think so?" I responded, feeling a lack of confidence in my knowledge of eastern European geography.

"Let's do it!" we both exclaimed together.

Three months later, we spent two weeks soaking up the dazzling Croatian coastline and towering Bosnian peaks with our friend Melody, who was living in the Croatian city of Osijek. Then, we parted ways for five days while I flew to Berlin for the Helsinki Consultation and Amy spent time touring Hungary. We met back up at Ben Gurion airport on July 5, Amy's birthday, where her close friend Erin also joined us.

We took a *sherut* (group taxi) to the House of Saints Simeon and Anne in downtown Jerusalem, the Franciscan monastery where Fr. David and his community lived and where he had invited us to stay. We showered and walked to Tmol Shilshom, my favorite little Jerusalem bookshop café, to celebrate Amy's birthday. The next day was Friday, the beginning of our first Shabbat (Sabbath) spent in Israel.

While I had grown accustomed to observing Shabbat back in Los Angeles, it feels entirely different to be in Israel for Shabbat. In Los Angeles (or anywhere else, for that matter), I was going against the grain of the dominant culture and surrounding society by observing Shabbat. Friday night was the most popular time to be out on the town, and the local bars, restaurants, and movie theaters were always packed.

I often felt like I was missing out on something by staying home (which I often did) on Friday nights. It was much better to be with Jewish or Messianic Jewish community on Shabbat, but because of urban sprawl and the diffuse nature of our community, meeting up on Shabbat (or even attending Ahavat Zion Messianic Synagogue) required navigating multiple freeways and often meant sitting in traffic for several hours.

This always struck me as both frustrating and ironic, as there are few things *less* restful than weekend Los Angeles traffic. So my options were to stay home by myself, in which case I missed out on the community aspect, or muscle through the exhausting traffic to be with friends and community.

Shabbat in Israel (and Jerusalem in particular), however, is an entirely different experience. You are going against the grain if you are attempting *not* to observe Shabbat. Shops and restaurants begin to close their doors on Friday afternoon, and you can literally walk down the middle of most streets for the next twenty-four hours, as driving on Shabbat is a rare thing to either do or see.

The Friday morning bustle is a weekly event in Israel: corner bakeries offering rows of freshly baked challah loaves on outside racks, butchers with their chopping blocks and glass display cases, fruit and vegetable stalls with bins of colorful produce piled high.

If you want the *full* Jerusalem Friday morning shopping experience, you can head to Machane Yehuda, where alley after alley of stalls offer not only meat, bread, fish, and produce, but where you will also find every flavor of halvah imaginable, as well as jewelry and scarves and roasted nuts and the best fish and chips you'll ever have in your life. But, be warned, you'll need to muster up your inner Israeli, for the alleys will be lined shoulder to shoulder and shopkeepers will be yelling things to one another and throwing items to each other that miss your head by just a few inches.

Native born Israelis are called *sabras*, which is a kind of cactus that grows throughout the Israeli countryside. The idea is that they're prickly and brusque on the outside, but soft and sweet on the inside. I've had to remind myself of this reality *many* times when in Israel; if I don't, the seeming rudeness and gruffness brings me to tears. "They're not yelling, Jen, they're just Israeli," I've often repeated to myself. You also learn very quickly that the concept of an orderly line doesn't exist in Israel; just push your way to the front or you'll be waiting for hours.

Amy, Erin, and I spent our first Shabbat with our Catholic friends in Jerusalem in the beautiful house where they were hosting us, trying to keep up with the conversation that quickly jumped from Hebrew to Polish to Italian with an occasional bit of English thrown in, exclusively for our sakes. We spent our second Shabbat in the quaint mountain town of Tiberias, where we stayed at a beautiful guest house overlooking the Sea of Galilee.

As the sun began to set, we sat together on the balcony above the terraced garden that led down to the water. Holding two braided challahs in my hands, I recited the traditional Jewish blessing over bread: *Baruch ata Adonai Eloheinu melech haʾolam hamotzi lechem min haʾaretz.* Blessed are you, Lord our God, King of the Universe, who brings forth bread from the earth.

ↄ•ↄ•ↄ

Perhaps the richest book on Shabbat is written by twentieth-century Jewish philosopher and rabbi, Abraham Joshua Heschel. Few books capture both the beauty and mystique of the essence of Shabbat like Heschel's. The central metaphor is architectural, and Heschel begins the book with the candid assertion that "technical civilization is man's conquest of space." While this conquest is part and parcel of humanity's commission in Genesis 1, the reality is that "the Bible is more concerned with time than with space."[1]

Shabbat draws us back into the realm of time, where we enter anew into the primary residence of holiness. In a "radical departure from accustomed religious thinking," the Genesis creation narrative does not endow anything material with holiness. The first thing to be declared holy is the Sabbath—a day, an institution in time. This primary locus of holiness grounds the institution of the holy people, Israel, and the eventual construction of a holy place, the temple. "The sanctity of time came first, the sanctity of man came second, and the sanctity of space last."[2]

To think about Shabbat in this light reveals a key difference in how it is understood in Judaism and Christianity. One phrase that always strikes me among my friends in Christian ministry is the idea that "Tuesday is my Sabbath," or "Thursday is my Sabbath,"

meaning that this is the day they disengage from ministry respon-
sibilities and spend time with family, or hiking, or going to the
movies, or otherwise recreating.

The thing is, in Judaism, Shabbat is Shabbat. You cannot observe
it whenever you want, because it exists independently, and it cannot
be moved to a day that fits better with our schedules. It will proceed,
with or without us present. It is something we enter into, not something we work into our busy schedule. In fact, in Judaism, one's
weekly schedule rotates around Shabbat. Shabbat is communal, and
the Jewish people observe it together.

As Heschel describes, the quality of time is different on Shabbat
than on the other days of the week. Heschel asks, "How should we
weigh the difference between the Sabbath and the other days of the
week? When a day like Wednesday arrives, the hours are blank, and
unless we lend significance to them, they remain without character.
The hours of the seventh day are significant in themselves; their
significance and beauty do not depend on any work, profit, or
progress we may achieve."[3]

Shabbat stands as a "palace in time,"[4] one that we are invited to
enter into and dwell in once a week. According to the ancient
rabbis, the labor we refrain from on Shabbat are the acts that were
necessary for constructing and furnishing the tabernacle. On
Shabbat, we are building into and investing in a sanctuary in time,
not a sanctuary in space.

However, the rest that is commanded on Shabbat is not merely,
or even primarily, a negative concept. The focus is not on what
we're giving up (work, productivity, technology, commerce, etc.),
but on what we are gaining. This reframe is illustrated by
Genesis 2:2, which tells us that "God completed—on the seventh
day—His work that He made, and He ceased—on the seventh day—
from all His work that He made" (TLV). The verse is confusing—if

God ceased from work on the seventh day, how could God still have been working?

According to Jewish tradition, God was actually still creating on the seventh day—God was creating rest (*menuha* in Hebrew), without which creation is incomplete. Menuha would become a signpost to eternity; in Judaism, the world to come is described as "the day that will be entirely Shabbat."[5] On Shabbat, we glimpse and taste eternity; it is as if, for this one day a week, we enter into another dimension of time.

ᔭ᛫ᔭ᛫ᔭ

As it turned out, the day after our Shabbat in Tiberias, Amy and Erin boarded our return flight without me. Just a few hours before our scheduled departure, I made the decision to extend my stay in order to spend a few extra days getting to know a man named Yonah.

I had been invited to give a lecture during our time in Jerusalem, and it was there that I first met Yonah. Our mutual friend Baruch told me about him just before the lecture, and Yonah and I were both among a small group of people who headed to a local sushi restaurant after the lecture ended. Before going our separate ways after dinner, Yonah asked for my number, and I awkwardly handed him my business card. "Uh, the cell number is the best way to reach me."

He texted two days later, and after a mix-up caused by poor cell reception, we met up for lunch. We sat on the soft grass in Independence Park in the center of Jerusalem and talked about our families and our dreams for the future, surrounded by the joyous laughter of kids playfully tagging one another and tumbling down the gentle slope.

I was intrigued by this brawny, quiet man who was so very different from me. His dark beard was longer than the neatly trimmed beards of men in my professional circles, and I was immediately attracted to the deep and pronounced crow's feet that appeared whenever he smiled. There was an evident humility about him, a lack of pretension and a certainty in who he was. I found myself wondering what it would be like to bring someone home to meet my parents whose head was adorned with a knitted *kippah* (yarmulke) and whose dangling tzitzit were clearly visible.

As we sat together in the park, I talked about my job search for a full-time tenure track teaching position, and he talked about his desire to be a father, a farmer, and a folk singer. The professional, formal, academic version of myself was subtly disarmed by his honesty and meekness. A few hours later, he walked me back to the monastery, and I felt sure I would never see him again.

That afternoon, Erin and Amy and I rented a car and drove from Jerusalem to Tiberias. I felt both a tinge of sadness and an overflowing sense of fullness as we drove up through the Jordan Valley; our time in Jerusalem had been incredibly meaningful, and the rich relationships we had cultivated there lingered and swirled around in my mind. The next day was Friday, and we drove to Tzfat to walk the narrow, cobbled streets and do our Shabbat shopping. On the way there, Yonah called.

"Any chance you would consider coming back to Jerusalem to spend Shabbat here?" he asked. I was flattered and surprised. Though I ended up staying in Tiberias, I spent much of Shabbat pondering our short phone conversation and Yonah's unexpected request.

When Shabbat ended on Saturday night, I texted Yonah. He ended up calling, and as I stood on the balcony of the guest house, watching moonlight reflect off the ripples on the Sea of Galilee, we shared about our Shabbats and talked about the weekly *parsha*, the section of Torah that Jews all over the world were reading that week. After a short pause in the conversation, Yonah asked if I would be willing to extend my stay in Israel.

I barely slept that night, and our flight back to the States was scheduled for the next evening. We woke up and embarked upon our last whirlwind touring day; Amy and Erin wanted to savor every last moment of sightseeing potential. We stopped at what felt like every significant site between Tiberias and Tel Aviv, with me waiting in the illegally parked car while they literally ran in and out of a dozen final "must sees." While they were snapping photos of famous churches and ancient Roman ruins, I was calling airlines and credit card companies, investigating the financial implications of extending my stay.

As Amy and Erin sprinted through Caesarea Maritima, I texted Yonah. "Can't change my flight for less than $1000." It was only a moment before the chime of his reply came through: "I'll pay for it."

Yonah owned a moving business with his brother Jake, and he had arranged to take the afternoon off so we could meet for a few final hours in Tel Aviv, while Amy and Erin took their last swim in the Mediterranean. Yonah took a bus to Tel Aviv, and we picked him up at Arlozorov Station and then headed to the beach. The situation felt surreal, and I couldn't seem to think clearly in the midst of it.

As the time came to meet back at the car, I realized that I would certainly regret not staying and seeing what might happen. It suddenly became crystal clear, and in the lobby of a high-rise beachfront hotel, I decided to stay. Yonah and I dropped Erin and Amy off at the airport and headed back to Jerusalem.

ɷ·ɷ·ɷ

Because the focus of Shabbat is not on what we're "giving up" due to prescribed restrictions but rather on what we are gaining by entering into the holiness of the day, we begin to see that the restrictions themselves are the portal into a deeper encounter with God.

In Heschel's words, "Sabbath is not an occasion for diversion or frivolity; not a day to shoot fireworks or to turn somersaults, but an opportunity to mend our tattered lives; to collect rather than to dissipate time. . . . Indeed, the prohibitions have succeeded in preventing the vulgarization of the grandeur of the day."[6] In our not watching Netflix or going to Starbucks or cleaning out the garage on Shabbat, we are preserving the sanctity of the day.

Furthermore, the concrete restrictions and prescriptions for Shabbat are what tether Shabbat to the realm of material existence, contra platonic dualism. Even as we peer into eternity on the seventh day, we do not escape from embodied existence in this world. As Heschel explains, "The Sabbath must always be in accord with actual deeds, with definite actions and abstentions."[7] On Shabbat we play on the carpet with our kids and eat specially prepared meals and take nature walks, experiencing the renewal of our bodies through time dedicated to the things that don't generally make it onto our to-do lists.

Shabbat rest is anchored in two key moments in the Bible: first, our rest mirrors God's own rest at the end of the creation process. "Remember the Sabbath day by keeping it holy," reads Exodus 20:8, where honoring the Sabbath is listed as the longest of the Ten Commandments. "For in six days the LORD made the heavens and the earth, the sea, and all that is in them, but he rested on the seventh day. Therefore the LORD blessed the Sabbath day and made it holy" (Exodus 20:11).

Rest is built into the created order and entering into it is one of the ways we live as image bearers of God. Though our weekday work is likely never actually done by the time Shabbat comes, we nonetheless set aside a day to commune with our God who taught us how to rest—regardless of what tasks we did or did not complete during the week. In this way, the weekday is relativized by Shabbat;

the work we do during the week yields to the rest we prioritize on Shabbat. If, as Augustine asserts, the work of faith is to properly order our loves, the commitment to Shabbat makes a clear statement about which mode of time orients our devotional life.

Second, our rest on Shabbat commemorates the exodus from Egypt, God's deliverance of his people Israel from brutal and soul-wrenching slavery. When the Ten Commandments are reiterated in Deuteronomy 5, this is the reason for the Sabbath commandment. "Remember that you were slaves in Egypt and that the LORD your God brought you out of there with a mighty hand and an out-stretched arm. Therefore the LORD your God has commanded you to observe the Sabbath day" (Deuteronomy 5:15).

According to Deuteronomy 5, our observance of the Sabbath is a weekly reminder that redemption is, in the end, God's work. This refrain is repeated again and again throughout Scripture. In the incredible story of the Israelites crossing the Red Sea, terrified by Pharaoh and his merciless army pursuing them, what are Moses' words to the panicking crowd? "Do not be afraid. Stand firm and you will see the deliverance the LORD will bring you today. The Egyptians you see today you will never see again. The LORD will fight for you; you need only to be still" (Exodus 14:13-14). This truth is most powerfully illustrated on the cross, where the ultimate triumph of good over evil was accomplished with no contribution on our part.

This repeated theme in the biblical narrative offers a fascinating and important caveat to what we discussed in the last chapter. While Judaism takes seriously humanity's vocation to usher in re-demption, it is never as though we are accomplishing this mighty task on our own. Our actions mirror and make manifest God's sovereign victory over the forces of death and darkness.

There's a saying in Judaism that "more than the Jewish people have kept Shabbat, Shabbat has kept the Jewish people." Indeed, Shabbat is one of the cornerstones of Jewish faith and life whose observance, over the centuries, has prevented the Jewish people from dissolving into the dominant cultures and societies within which they have almost always dwelt. This reality offers a sobering word to us about the power of our practices and habits in living out our vocation as the people of God.

‹ɔ·ɔ·ɔ

So what happened? Why is the Jewish Shabbat so distant from mainstream Christian worship and discipleship? While Sunday worship (built upon the foundation of the resurrection) is present in the New Testament, the final split between Judaism's Shabbat and Christianity's practice of worshiping on Sunday is embedded within the complexities of the parting of the ways between Judaism and Christianity.[8]

One window into this development is the *Epistle of Barnabas*, likely composed just before the Bar Kochba revolt in the early second century and focused on the reality of Judaism and Christianity increasingly becoming two separate and mutually exclusive communities. *Barnabas* argues that Jews and Christians do not share a common covenant with God, and that the Jewish people's commitment to Jewish practice (including the Sabbath) reveals their inability to understand the true core of God's covenant love and lays bare their blind eyes, hard hearts, and evil deceptions.

Barnabas offers commentary on God's chastisement in Isaiah 1:13 ("New Moons, Sabbaths and convocations—I cannot bear your worthless assemblies"), concluding that God is instead calling Christians to "keep the eighth day as a day of gladness, on which also Jesus rose from the dead, and after he had appeared ascended unto heaven."[9] Here it is clear that, by this point in history, Christian worship on Sunday was a deliberate act of dissociation from any connection to the Jewish people and Jewish practice.

Once Constantine became emperor in AD 306, he issued a series of laws that permitted and facilitated Christian Sunday worship. Indeed, Constantine was a major player in the parting of the ways. While his endorsement of Sunday worship was likely due to his own identification with the growing Christian movement (as well as its convenient overlap with the pagan day of sun worship, which also retained significance for Constantine), his actions contributed to the widening rift between the largely Gentile Christian community throughout the Roman Empire and the Jewish people. Here again we see Jewish followers of Jesus positioned as the crumbling bridge of the excluded middle.

What does all of this mean for Christians today? From my perspective, Christians do not have the same relationship with the Jewish Shabbat as Jews do, nor should they feel obligated to observe the Sabbath on the day or in the way Jews do. In fact, the establishment of Sunday as the Christian day of worship has become a mainstay of Christianity in a way that has secured this day as a key time for fellowship, worship, and mutual enrichment.

What I think Christians can learn from a deeper understanding of the Jewish Shabbat is a kind of *sabbath ethic*, which every single person of faith can benefit from. The contours of the Jewish Shabbat can serve as a challenge about how Christians prioritize their time and resources, and perhaps a nudge to consider taking one day per week as a time of intentional reflection, or personal retreat, or quality family time.

Additionally, understanding the Jewish Shabbat is part of understanding the fabric of Jewish life, essentially helping Christians to understand the religious lifeblood of their covenantal forebears.

Hopefully, putting Shabbat in a particular light can also serve to help dismantle the all-too-common Christian stereotypes about Jewish legalism and rote religiosity.

It is also worth mentioning that Sunday, the Lord's Day, has something profound to teach us about the life of faith. The early Jesus-following community began to gather and worship on Sunday precisely because this was the day that Jesus rose from the dead. While the eventual sharp distinction between the Jewish Shabbat and the Christian Lord's Day became politicized and polarizing, this basic fact cannot be overlooked. Jesus' first followers recognized that something incredible, something cosmic, had happened on the Sunday following Jesus' brutal crucifixion, something that changed the course of history and points toward our own ultimate destiny. Our challenge, then, is to embrace both the inherent richness and beauty of Shabbat in Judaism while recognizing the fundamental novelty that the Lord's Day commemorates.[10]

~·~·~

For me, Shabbat has become a gift that gives itself anew each week. No matter how chaotic any given week has been, I know that Shabbat will be waiting with open arms. It truly feels like a different quality of time than "ordinary" time; it is elevated time, in every sense of the word.

No glaring screens, no ringing phones, no TVs on in the background, no music playing, no checking email. Nothing from the workday world clamoring for attention. Sitting down for lingering meals, no checking watches. Conversations that are allowed to wander and wind for as long as they please. Morning walks through sparkling sunlight passing between tree branches. Afternoons spent relaxing in a park with a good book and an iced tea.

The rich time with friends and family that typifies Shabbat stands next to another feature of Shabbat, a quieter and sometimes unsettling feature. Amid the joy of being able to breathe freely, to-do lists tucked away until Sunday morning, Shabbat uncovers and names our reliance upon (and addiction to?) the hum and busyness of the week. The pressing demands and deadlines have a numbing quality, dutifully preventing us from quieting our minds long enough for the more difficult thoughts to arise. The uncertainty, the fears, the losses. The open arms of Shabbat do not discriminate; they provide space for the sweetness of connection and relationship but also for sadness and longing to surface. It all meets there, in the one sacred day of rest and, sometimes, restlessness.

Of course, even this more fragile and vulnerable aspect of Shabbat is of great value. It reveals that the more we run away from and attempt to silence the dark and haunting thoughts, the more power they actually gain. There is a certain freedom in stopping our intentionally endless hustling, turning around, and looking at them square in the face. Taking the time to be with them, to study their contours rather than running from them allows us to build a relationship with them rather than being consumed by them. And so, though painful, these hard and threatening aspects of Shabbat's quiet are also part of the sowing of our souls.

9

THE SPIRIT

I will put my Spirit in you and move you to follow
my decrees and be careful to keep my laws.

<small>EZEKIEL 36:27</small>

A s Amy and Erin were arriving back in Los Angeles, Yonah and I met in Zion Square and headed to Even Sapir where we would spend the day hiking the Israel Trail and continuing to get to know each other. I was only able to extend my stay by three days, as I had committed months prior to guest preaching at a church in Lake Tahoe that Sunday. Yonah was thus co-opted into my sermon prep, which would now be done in Israel as opposed to back in Los Angeles. In the middle of our hike, we sat at a picnic table over-looking the Jerusalem forest and read through the Gospel of Mark from beginning to end.

"Would you like to meet my family tonight?" Yonah asked as we hiked back toward the car. "Of course," I responded, without hesitation. After all, we lived across the world from one another and only had two and a half more days together—why wouldn't I want to pile on the added pressure and potential of meeting the family?!

Yonah was born in the United States and raised as part of the Messianic Jewish movement in Virginia, and his family had always embraced a strong Zionist ideology. As I was moving into the dorms as a freshman in college, Yonah was moving to Israel to pursue the dream he had been cultivating since he was a small child. He was the first in his family to make *aliyah* (a Hebrew word meaning "to go up," this is the term used when a Jew immigrates to Israel), and his parents and Jake's family would soon follow. Jake and his wife Sarah now had seven children, and the entire family (as well as Sarah's parents and two of her brothers) lived in a small suburb just north of Jerusalem. Though Yonah held both American and Israeli citizenship, he considered himself permanently established in Israel; when we met, he hadn't been back to the United States in eight years.

Yonah and I picked up falafel and shawarma for the whole family and met up with them in Park Haggai, where I was immediately drawn into the warmth and closeness of his family. We ate dinner on the outside patio at Jake and Sarah's, and something about the dynamic of this family I had just met felt like home to me. The girls took me into their room after dinner to show me their beading collection, and Yonah's dad gave me a brief agricultural lesson on the trees that shaded the backyard.

After two more very full days, Yonah drove me back to the airport and we said goodbye in the middle of a crowded hallway just before I went through security. "Call me when you land," Yonah said, reluctantly letting go of my hand as we parted.

On my fifteen-hour flight back to the States, I mentally replayed every detail of the last week; it felt as though my mental fixation on it was the only thing keeping it all real. As the hours of the flight passed and my return to life in Los Angeles drew closer, my thoughts shifted to the theological realm.

Yonah and his family lived immersed in wider Jewish Israeli culture, a far cry from my evangelical Christian Fuller Seminary community. Yes, I was inching my way deeper into the Messianic Jewish world, but even that felt like something entirely different from the life Yonah was living.

This would prove to be one of the most difficult aspects of our long-distance dating relationship; each time we would visit each other, the gaping incongruity between our separate lives would threaten to topple the relationship and the dreams and desires we held in common. Yonah felt utterly out of place in my world of Christian higher education and academic theology, and I began to feel as though life with him and the life I had been building before I met him somehow translated into a zero-sum game.

The complexity of it all continued to permeate my theological ruminations as well. How could the same Spirit infuse both the Vineyard model of "doing the stuff" that had so influenced my spiritual development since college *and* the wholly Jewish, Torah-observant rhythms that Yonah and his Jerusalem community lived within?[1] I decided to tackle this topic for my presentation at the following year's Helsinki Consultation meeting, which was to be held in Oslo, Norway.

ᔕ•ᔕ•ᔕ

According to Mark Kinzer's Messianic Jewish theology, being a follower of Jesus looks different for Jews than it does for Gentiles. Kinzer calls this "bilateral ecclesiology," meaning that there are two parts of the *ekklēsia*, or body of Christ. For Jews, following Messiah means living out the contours of God's enduring covenant with Israel, believing Jesus to be the climax of the covenant and the ultimate model of covenant fidelity. For Gentiles, following Jesus does not require adherence to Jewish practice or tradition. Kinzer points to key passages in the New Testament that affirm this configuration, but that in most cases have been understood otherwise on account of the history of Christian biblical interpretation.[2]

As I wrote my paper for the next Helsinki Consultation, I questioned whether Kinzer's notion of bilateral ecclesiology might also apply to other areas of theological reflection. Particularly, I began to wonder if the coming of the Spirit might mean something different for Jews than for Gentiles.

In asking this question, it must be made clear that *unity* among the twofold body of Messiah cannot be neglected or downgraded in any way. To forsake unity would be to undermine the thrust of the entire New Testament and essentially rebuild the "dividing wall" that Paul assures us has been torn down through Christ (Ephesians 2:14). Kinzer is not attempting to question or challenge this unity; rather, he is committed to pointing out that unity, in this case, was never intended to equal uniformity. It is within this unwavering commitment to unity that I began to explore these questions about the Holy Spirit.

My starting point for pressing into a Messianic Jewish pneumatology (doctrine of the Spirit) was the assertion that the gift of the Spirit reinforces the contours of Israel's particular vocation, while also making a way for Gentiles to enter into covenantal relationship with God and God's people. What, I wondered, might the coming of the Spirit mean for Jewish followers of Messiah?

The Pentecost narrative in Acts 2 occurs during the Jewish festival of Shavuot, an important detail that offers necessary context for understanding the coming of the Spirit. In Hebrew, Shavuot means "weeks," and refers to the seven weeks between the exodus from Egypt and God's revelation of the Ten Commandments on

Mount Sinai. Greek-speaking Jews referred to Shavuot as Pentecost (the "fiftieth" day, i.e., seven weeks).

According to a Jewish tradition which was likely already known in the first century, Shavuot commemorates the day on which God gave the Torah to the Israelites, and it is one of the three pilgrimage festivals in Judaism (along with Passover and Sukkot); this explains why, in Acts 2:5, "there were staying in Jerusalem God-fearing Jews from every nation under heaven." The imagery of the Acts 2 Pentecost account parallels the Exodus 19–20 narrative of God's giving of the Ten Commandments at Sinai. Exodus 19:16 refers to "thunder and lightning, with a thick cloud over the mountain, and a very loud trumpet blast." Similarly, Acts 2:2-3 refers to "a sound like the blowing of a violent wind," and "what seemed to be tongues of fire."

In order to unpack these parallels between Shavuot (i.e., the giving of the Torah) and Pentecost (i.e., the giving of the Spirit), we first must look at the tight connection between the giving of the Torah and the exodus from Egypt. In Israel's history and theology, these events are two sides of the same coin; they are the two essential steps to Israel gaining freedom. But what does this freedom look like?

In popular Western parlance, freedom is instinctively understood as "freedom to," which implies a lack of constraint and the ability to self-determine. This kind of freedom is tantamount to *liberty*, which, for example, the United States Declaration of Independence promises to protect as an "inalienable right," and which American citizens uphold as a fundamental value.

This notion, however, does not capture the essence of biblical freedom. From a scriptural perspective, autonomous self-determination is the sure path to ruin. Israel's story repeatedly illustrates the way in which the people's corporate life is dependent upon a certain yieldedness to the will and ways of God. Biblical freedom is more aptly categorized as "freedom from" rather than "freedom to"; it is not so much *liberty* as it is *liberation*.[3] Obedience and submission to God is the singular path to freedom from the many false gods that vie for our loyalty and promise an abundant life. Israel's history testifies to the way in which straying from obedience to God inevitably leads to idolatry.

This biblical notion of freedom undergirds the theological significance of the Exodus-Sinai event. As Rabbi Donin explains, "The festival of Shavuot emphasizes the spiritually significant lesson that the release from bondage and the winning of political freedom does not constitute complete freedom unless it culminates in the spiritual *restraints, disciplines, and duties* inherent in the Revelation to Israel and in Israel's acceptance of the Torah."[4]

If the Israelites had been liberated from Egypt only to pursue their own earthly desires, they would have merely traded one cruel master for another. In other words, if the exodus is about Israel gaining freedom, that freedom is incomplete and misdirected without Torah.

Because Torah is intimately connected to freedom, and because the coming of the Spirit occurs during Israel's annual celebration of the giving of the Torah, we can affirm with Paul that "where the Spirit of the Lord is, there is freedom" (2 Corinthians 3:17). We must remember, however, that this freedom does not mean a lack of constraint or restraint. It is characterized by communal structure, order, and submission to God. The Spirit thus enables the people of God to faithfully journey onward, providing the community with the same kinds of "restraints, disciplines, and duties" that Israel had always known through the Torah.

In fact, for Israel, the coming of the Spirit is indeed correlated with the empowerment to obey Torah. During the Babylonian exile, Ezekiel's prophetic promise of restoration envisions a time when

God will regather his people from the nations where they have been scattered and bring them back into the land of Israel (Ezekiel 11:17). Ezekiel continues: "They will return to it and remove all its vile images and detestable idols. I will give them an undivided heart and put a new spirit in them; I will remove from them their heart of stone and give them a heart of flesh. Then they will follow my decrees and be careful to keep my laws. They will be my people, and I will be their God" (Ezekiel 11:18-20).

Again, in chapter 36, Ezekiel prophesies Israel's return to the Promised Land and voices God's promise: "I will give you a new heart and put a new spirit in you; I will remove from you your heart of stone and give you a heart of flesh. And I will put my Spirit in you and move you to follow my decrees and be careful to keep my laws. Then you will live in the land I gave your ancestors; you will be my people, and I will be your God" (Ezekiel 36:26-28). According to Ezekiel's vision of restoration, the land, obedience to Torah, and the gift of God's Spirit go hand in hand.[5]

From this perspective, the people of Israel's obedience to the Torah is enabled by the divine empowerment brought by God's Spirit. While Messiah provides atonement for sins and models the perfect fulfillment of Torah, the gift of his Spirit enables Christ's disciples to follow in his footsteps. By the power of the Spirit, Israel is thus empowered to faithfully live out the life to which it is called, a life of obedience and submission to God.

ᔕ•ᔕ•ᔕ

Yonah and I had met in July, and he flew out to California for Sukkot (the Feast of Tabernacles) in September. We spent the first half of our time in Pasadena, and I purchased my first ever *sukkah*[6] from a small store in the San Fernando Valley the week before he arrived. Yonah guest lectured in my undergraduate theology classes ("You cannot share my water bottle today; we have to make this look professional!" I coached him as we arrived on campus), and halfway through Sukkot we strapped the disassembled sukkah to the top of my SUV and drove to Tahoe, where we would spend the next several days with my family.

After I became a follower of Jesus in college, my parents had begun investigating the claims of Christianity, mostly to try to prove me (and my brother) wrong. The pastor of the Vineyard church I was attending had given me a book to pass along to my dad; the book was called *Betrayed!* and the subtitle was *How Do You Feel When You Are Successful, 50 and Jewish, and Your 21-Year-Old Daughter Tells You She Believes in Jesus?*[7] This was, basically, our exact situation. My dad read the book with fervor, and despite his intentions, he became overwhelmed by what he perceived as undeniable truth in the claims of Jesus. His attachment to Judaism was never very strong, and he was intrigued by this Messiah who wasn't afraid to critique religiosity and who fostered a sense of personal connection to God.

My mom was devastated when my brother and I first told her about our faith in Jesus, and she indeed felt a sense of betrayal. She blamed herself for not instilling in us a deep enough sense of Jewish identity, and she immediately reached out to the rabbi of her youth for guidance. In the end, while her journey included considerably more wrestling and grappling than my dad's, she too had come to confess faith in Jesus. My parents became involved in a local church, and though my mom would often remark that she felt more of a natural connection with her secular Jewish friends than these Gentile evangelical Christians, they have increasingly found their spiritual home in this particular Christian community. Over the years, I have felt inexpressibly grateful that my own commitment to Jesus has not caused an enduring rift in my immediate family, which is by far the more common scenario in Jewish families.

Now, as Yonah and I pulled into the driveway, both of my parents descended the steps from the front door to greet us. Our relationship was, after all, the talk of our small town.

While my family couldn't help but fall in love with Yonah's kind spirit and evident gentleness, he was not quite met with the same open arms with which I was immediately received into his family. He was committed to living in Israel, which my family understandably perceived as a huge threat to our tight-knit family structure. They weren't alone in this struggle, either. For me, it was the single most intense aspect of the long process of discernment that dating Yonah hurled me into. I wasn't raised with the same kind of Zionist zeal as Yonah, and I began questioning for the first time whether or not I could envision myself in Israel long-term.

Upon our arrival in Tahoe, Yonah was presented with a six-page, seventeen-question document that my dad had composed in advance of a private lunch he had requested to have with Yonah. The questions ranged from "What are your philosophies regarding family structure and gender roles?" to "Are you financially able to support a wife and family?" to "Are you concerned about raising a family in a country marked for extinction by its neighbors?"

I couldn't help but be reminded of an entirely comical "Application to Date My Daughter" that had circulated the internet a number of years prior. But this was no joke. Thank the good Lord that my brother ended up joining the private lunch, serving as a kind of referee throughout the tense conversation (so I'm told). He blew the whistle when my dad tried to interrupt Yonah's carefully formulated responses to the absolutely impossible set of questions and, in some cases, declared aspects of my dad's interrogation to be patently out of bounds.

As my dad would later describe, Yonah was wholly undaunted by my dad's best intimidation and deterrent tactics. "He made it clear that he was going to just step right around me," my dad would recall with a smirk on his face. "He wanted to marry my daughter, and I quickly saw that I wasn't going to dissuade him." Though our relationship has undoubtedly had its share of twists and turns, my parents would be the first to admit that Yonah's measured disposition and deep well of faithfulness offer the best possible complement and antidote to my fleeting yet strong emotions and my tendency to live in the world of worst-case scenarios.

I spent the month of December in a very rainy Israel, and Yonah came back to California for Passover in April. In the intervening months we thanked God for cheap international calling plans, and I spent many nights being awakened midsleep cycle by Yonah's calls before he headed off to work. A ten-hour time difference is, in my estimation, among the most difficult to navigate.

Every time we visited each other our relationship was tested almost to a breaking point. I can't count the number of park benches I sat on while crying (um, awkward). I vividly recall at least a dozen agonizing episodes over the course of that year when I was convinced things were ending, and I began to enter into the messy and all-consuming routine of grieving what we almost had.

And yet, even as our differences threatened to unravel our connection, we continually managed to work through them and come back together. Yonah was diligent to point out when I was treating our relationship like a spreadsheet whose calculations weren't quite adding up. He persistently tempered my sense that we needed to thoroughly work out every future hypothetical detail in advance.

My brother begged me not to make any major life decisions before spending three months in the same place as Yonah, which seemed like sage advice. I disentangled myself from all commitments in Los

Angeles for the following summer, and Yonah found me a tiny studio apartment just a block away from where he was living.

Once again, as the heat of summer set in, I boarded a plane to Israel. Yonah picked me up at the airport, flowers in hand, and, after stopping by the grocery store, we headed to my apartment. When we got there, we found his parents literally scrubbing the place down, as they had just that afternoon gotten the keys. Amid a cloud of bleach, his dad gave me a big hug, stepped back for a moment, then gave me another big hug. "It's just so good to see you, Jen!" he exclaimed through his Santa Claus-like beard.

ᘯ·ᘯ·ᘯ

If the coming of the Spirit empowers Jewish followers of Jesus to live out a life of faithful obedience to the Torah, the next question becomes, "What might the gift of the Spirit mean for Gentile followers of Jesus?"

Acts 3–9 includes numerous references to the Spirit's presence and power among the believing community and Acts 10 tells the story of the surprising inclusion of Gentiles in this ever-expanding movement of God. When Peter recounts the narrative of God's work in Christ at Cornelius's house, after both Peter and Cornelius have received visions from God, "the Holy Spirit came on all who heard the message" (Acts 10:44). Peter and his Jewish companions "were astonished that the gift of the Holy Spirit had been poured out even on Gentiles" (Acts 10:45). In this regard, the Spirit indeed extends the work of Messiah; God's presence and holiness continue to expand outward, astounding even those Jews who had followed Jesus and had been participating in his mission. Apparently, they had not yet realized the full implications of the outward expansion of God's reign of which they themselves were a part.

The presence of the Spirit among both Jews and Gentiles illustrates what it actually means that the "dividing wall" has been torn down. In Peter's vision in Acts 10, he is instructed "not to call impure anything that God has made clean" (Acts 10:15). Peter's understanding of this vision has everything to do with fellowship between Jews and Gentiles (and *not* with eating nonkosher animals), as evidenced by the interpretation he offers in Acts 11 and Acts 15. In Acts 11, the response of the Jewish believers to Peter's explanation is, "So then, God has granted even the Gentiles repentance unto life" (Acts 11:18 BSB).

Indeed, it is precisely the gift of the Spirit that creates and concretizes unity and fellowship between Jews and Gentiles. Three times in the book of Acts, it is noted that the Spirit came upon the Gentiles *just as the Spirit came upon the Jews* (Acts 10:47, 11:15, 15:8-9). This, for the Jewish believers, was the overwhelming proof that God's work extended beyond the people of Israel.

However, it is determined early on that the *implications* of the gift of the Spirit—and of God's presence and work—are not the same for Jews as for Gentiles. This is the issue that occasions the Jerusalem council in Acts 15, and the fact that the Spirit came upon the Gentiles *as Gentiles* constitutes Peter's argument that Gentiles need not be required to obey all the commandments of the Torah. While the Spirit's presence among both Jews and Gentiles powerfully illustrates and actualizes God's ever-expanding work in the world, it apparently does not erase the distinction— particularly with regard to stipulations of covenant faithfulness— between Jew and Gentile.

While the Spirit empowers Jews to uphold the "restraints, disciplines, and duties" to which the Torah had always called them, the Spirit likewise orders the lives of Gentile followers of Jesus *so that* they may live as the people of God alongside and joined to the people of Israel. The practices that are required of Gentile believers in Acts 15 illustrate their turn from idolatry and arguably set basic parameters that enable table fellowship between Jews and Gentiles. Through God's work in their midst, Gentiles join into Israel's corporate life without themselves becoming Jews.

This democratization of the Spirit illustrates the ever-widening expansion of God's work and presence and establishes a solid bridge between Jews and Gentiles within the people of God. This bridge does not erase distinction but rather facilitates and enables intimate fellowship among those whose covenantal callings look different in practice. Like Kinzer's bilateral ecclesiology, this portrayal of bilateral pneumatology illustrates the way in which God's redemptive and consummative work empowers both Jews and Gentiles to carry out a life of obedience, uniquely but jointly.

In the words of Paul, "We were all baptized by one Spirit so as to form one body—whether Jews or Gentiles, slave or free—and we were all given the one Spirit to drink" (1 Corinthians 12:13). It is the Spirit who binds the twofold body of Christ together, and this unity must be preserved even as Jewish and Gentile followers of Jesus live faithfully within the unique contours of their respective redemptive vocations.

∽·∽·∽

I presented these ideas at the Helsinki Consultation in Oslo, and, as expected, the theological dialogue with friends whose companionship I so deeply cherish was a true gift. The most significant part of my time in Oslo, however, came unexpectedly.

It was there, as I spent time with this group of dear friends, that I gained the unmistakable clarity I had been seeking for a year on my relationship with Yonah. On the second evening, as I said goodnight to the rest of the group and headed to my small room in the monastery where we were staying, a profound realization materialized. It had the same gravity as my hearing from God about the Birthright trip; it was clear, unmistakable, and proved to be grounding in a way that even my intellect couldn't dismantle.

What I realized with utter lucidity was that the most abundant life I could imagine would be lived out in Israel, with Yonah by my side. The clarity came amid yet another episode of disconnect and strain between us, and our last communication had been a tense conversation from Heathrow Airport in London as I waited for my flight to Oslo.

One of our biggest issues was related to timeframe. Yonah was accustomed to the Orthodox Jewish world, where dating and courtship is a relatively short and straightforward process; it is often only a couple of months from the time a couple meets to the time they are engaged (or even married). I was coming from more of a modern Western model, and my friends were encouraging me that time was on my side and not to rush into anything. We both felt that getting more invested in one another if our relationship wasn't going to end in marriage was undesirable, but our approaches to handling that issue were opposite. For him, the sooner we got married, the better. For me, I couldn't get engaged before having the kind of absolute clarity that finally came in Oslo.

As the realization about abundant life continued to set in, I sat on my bed in the corner of the small room and wrote Yonah an email. "It's hard to explain all the things I've been thinking about here, mostly about how much I miss you and am longing to be with you . . . for the rest of my life." Despite our challenges and differences, perhaps the same Spirit who holds together Jew and Gentile could likewise hold together Yonah and me.

10

SACRED DAYS

Place me like a seal over your heart, like a seal on your arm;
for love is as strong as death, its jealousy unyielding as the grave.
It burns like blazing fire, like a mighty flame.

SONG OF SONGS 8:6

When the conference in Oslo ended, I headed back to Israel. My time with Yonah felt qualitatively different upon my return to Jerusalem, and the clarity I had experienced proved lasting and real. What had started as a summer in Israel increasingly became an opportunity to settle into a future life there, and to begin planning out the logistic contours of that life. On August 3, we went ring shopping on Jaffa Street in downtown Jerusalem, and on August 10, Yonah proposed on the beach at Herzliya against the backdrop of crashing waves rolling white onto the sandy shore.

We scheduled our wedding for a mere seven weeks later, in my parents' backyard in Lake Tahoe, hoping there wouldn't be an early snowstorm that fall. I began a new routine of talking to my mom every morning on my daily walk, and together we planned out every detail of the wedding over the phone. Her best friend accompanied her to cake tastings and meetings with the wedding planner in my absence, and on September 1, I flew back to Los Angeles. I spent a blissful two weeks with friends, sold everything I owned, and celebrated my last Jewish High Holidays with the community at Ahavat Zion Messianic Synagogue.

During my doctoral program, I had begun a tradition of reading over a particular section of *The Star of Redemption* each year on Yom Kippur, the Day of Atonement. *The Star of Redemption*, whose dense content was penned on postcards in the trenches in World War I, is the magnum opus of twentieth-century German Jewish philosopher Franz Rosenzweig. Here Rosenzweig lays out the most comprehensive and complementary construal of Judaism and Christianity that has ever been written.

Rosenzweig includes detailed flourishes about the theological significance of Jewish and Christian holidays, and the way each of them symbolically enacts the movements of creation, revelation and redemption, events that provide the structure of his entire theological system. On Yom Kippur I would read over his reflections on the meaning of this day, and this particular year—a mere two weeks before my wedding—I was struck in an entirely different way than any other time I'd read it.

As I entered into the difficult afternoon hours of the Yom Kippur fast, I was powerfully moved by Rosenzweig's discussion of the garment that is traditionally worn by men (and, in some Jewish circles, by women as well) on Yom Kippur. In general, it is traditional to wear white on Yom Kippur and, in particular, to wear a white garment called a *kittel*.

Like everything in Judaism, the significance of this act is layered. A kittel is the traditional Jewish burial garment; wearing it on Yom Kippur represents the Jewish people's collective guilt before God, which is a main focus of this day. God cannot abide unholiness and impurity, and on Yom Kippur the Jewish people must stare in the face of their own sinfulness and shortcomings. "Forgive us, pardon us, atone for us," the Yom Kippur liturgy repeatedly pleads. The Day of Atonement is a day of judgment, where each individual Jew (and the Jewish people collectively) must reckon with the weight of their sin and culpability before God.

However, wearing a kittel also represents the miracle of God's forgiveness, another key theme of Yom Kippur. To don a kittel is to visually embody the notion that "though your sins are like scarlet, they shall be as white as snow" (Isaiah 1:18). For Rosenzweig, Yom Kippur is thus profoundly a day of both life and death. In place of death as a result of sin, God grants the people lavish forgiveness and the gift of continued life. One is not without the other, and each lends meaning to its opposite.

After poignantly describing the significance of wearing a kittel on Yom Kippur, Rosenzweig references Song of Songs 8:6, where we read that "love is as strong as death." Rosenzweig continues: "And this is why the individual already once in life wears the full burial dress: under the wedding canopy, after he has received it on his wedding day from the hands of the bride."[1]

This was precisely the part that caused my breath to catch in my throat that particular year. I had read it many times before, but never with the same gravity of meaning. Death and new life, sin and forgiveness, repentance and pardon—these key themes surrounding Yom Kippur are also the daily pathways of marriage, a reality I would experience profoundly in the years to come.

In fact, according to Jewish tradition, one's wedding day is like one's own personal Yom Kippur, and certain traditional practices reflect this correlation. Many Jews fast on their wedding day, as Jews across the world fast on Yom Kippur; certain prayers that are designated for Yom Kippur are also recited on one's wedding day; finally, while it is traditional for a Jewish man to wear a kittel on his wedding day, the bride is, of course, traditionally wearing a white dress. The power of these images swirled around in my mind as I sat there that day, feeling the hunger pangs of the Yom Kippur fast and preparing to marry Yonah.

Notably, there is one more occasion in the Jewish calendar when a kittel is traditionally worn—during the annual Passover seder, especially by the one leading the seder. On that particular Yom Kippur, I was left pondering the connection not only between Yom Kippur and one's wedding day, but also between Yom Kippur and Passover.

∽·∽·∽

Many of these theologically rich connections have been lost as Judaism and Christianity increasingly distanced themselves from one another, rending the very threads that once interwove the deeply meaningful rhythms of the liturgical year.

As we seek to press into the link between Yom Kippur and Passover, it is helpful to begin with a bit of background for each.[2] Yom Kippur is instituted in the Torah (specifically in Leviticus 16, Leviticus 23:26-32, and Numbers 29:7-11) and falls on the tenth day of the seventh month of the Hebrew calendar, the month of Tishrei. Tishrei is preceded by Elul, and the entirety of Elul is focused on the theme of repentance. The first day of Tishrei is Rosh Hashanah, the Jewish New Year, which begins the Ten Days of Awe, a kind of elevated and heightened mini season in the Jewish calendar.

According to Jewish tradition, the forty-day period of repentance from the beginning of Elul to the tenth of Tishrei corresponds to the forty days Moses interceded for the people of Israel after the sin of the golden calf. In Exodus 32, while Moses was atop

Mount Sinai receiving the two stone tablets from God, the people grew anxious and impatient and fashioned an idol to worship—an event that stands out as one of Israel's greatest affronts before God. Upon descending into the camp and seeing the people dancing around the golden calf, Moses throws down the stone tablets, shattering them at the foot of the mountain. It is an utter low point in Israel's history, where the depth of their sin and guilt before God seems irreparable.

And yet, in an overwhelmingly poignant story, God reveals his glory to Moses who stands in a cleft in a rock and fashions a new set of stone tablets. In an act of sheer unmerited grace, God renews the covenant with his people, declaring that he is "the LORD, the compassionate and gracious God, slow to anger, abounding in love and faithfulness, maintaining love to thousands, and forgiving wickedness, rebellion and sin" (Exodus 34:6-7). After remaining on the mountain for forty days and forty nights, Moses again descends into the camp, face radiant.

According to the rabbis, this event is the birth of Yom Kippur, the day that represents both the height of the people's sin and iniquity and at the same time the depth of God's unfailing love and unmerited forgiveness. This is the grand story the Jewish people enter into each year, clothed in white and ever in need of divine mercy and grace.

The story of Passover (*Pesach* in Hebrew) fills the Exodus narrative just before the people's arrival at Mount Sinai. As part of the Israelites' divine rescue from the shackles of slavery under Pharaoh, God brings ten plagues on the Egyptians. Before the tenth plague (the death of the firstborn son) commences, God tells Moses to instruct each Israelite family to slaughter a lamb and use its blood to mark the doorposts and lintel of their homes. The spirit of destruction, tasked with taking the life of every firstborn son, sees the blood on the entrance of the Israelite houses and *passes over* them, sparing Israel's firstborn sons.

According to God's instruction, Moses decrees that Israel is to observe the Pesach feast each year, and so, to this day, Jews faithfully gather for this most sacred meal on the fourteenth day of the first month, the month of Nisan (Exodus 12). The table is adorned with special elements and foods, all of which play a role in remembering—literally, tasting—the experience of that fateful night, and of the ensuing sojourn through the Sinai wilderness. Israel thus forever commemorates that on the darkest night in the recorded history of Egypt, the flesh and blood of a lamb marked— and saved—the children of Abraham, Isaac, and Jacob.

During the annual Passover seder, the Jewish people reenact and confront once again the pains of slavery, the tears of despair, and even the cries of the Egyptians. But we also commemorate the triumph of liberation, the joy of new beginnings, the mystery of God's power and love, and the hope of someday making a proper home in the Promised Land.

As all four Gospels make clear, Passover serves as the backdrop of Jesus' entry into Jerusalem, his "last supper" with his disciples, and ultimately his death and resurrection. Constantine at the Council of Nicaea decreed to decouple Easter from Passover, a decision that set into motion a long process of wiping away the Jewish roots of Holy Week. In order to press into and rediscover these rich and foundational connections, what is needed is not merely reclaiming the link between Passover and Easter, but also incorporating Yom Kippur into our understanding of Holy Week.

∽·∽·∽

In Rosenzweig's thought, as well as in Jewish tradition more generally, a tallit is symbolic of a kittel. It is also traditionally white, and though generally only worn in the daytime, the one exception to this is the eve of Yom Kippur, when it is worn after the sun has set. In fact, it is traditional to wear it the entire day during Yom Kippur.

Many Jewish men do not own or wear a tallit until after they are married, and it is traditional for the bride to gift the groom a tallit (rather than a kittel) on their wedding day. Yonah held to this tradition, and before heading back to the States, we went to the Ramot mall outside Jerusalem and picked out a beautiful tallit that I gave him as part of our wedding ceremony.[3]

Our wedding included many traditional Jewish elements, which no doubt provided quite a crosscultural religious education for the many Christian guests in attendance. Mark Kinzer officiated, gently guiding those present through the various elements of the ceremony. He and Yonah stood under the *chuppah* (traditional Jewish marriage canopy, representing the bride and groom's new home together with God's presence as their covering) where I, after being walked down the aisle, circled Yonah seven times in accordance with Jewish tradition. The ceremony included a public gifting of the tallit, a public reading of our *ketubah* (marriage contract), and the traditional breaking of the glass at the end. This act is done as a symbolic reminder that even in life's most joyous moments we still carry with us the pain and tragedy of Jewish history, most specifically the two historical destructions of the Jerusalem temple.

Our entire wedding weekend was a beautiful blur, with events that began on Friday evening and wrapped up with breakfast on Monday morning. In actuality, the whole thing was a wedding-slash-going-away-party, which, for the record, I do not recommend. Friends and family had flown in from around the country, and what I so desperately wanted was to pause time and spend an hour of one-on-one time with each of them. I imagine that many brides feel this way, and my experience was heightened by the fact that, exactly one week later, I would board a plane for Israel and begin an entirely new life there. The weekend was utterly exhausting for my introverted now-husband, who, whenever the topic comes up, jokingly asks, "Was I at our wedding?"

After the Monday morning breakfast, Yonah and I drove to Monterey, California, where my parents had arranged for us to spend the week. We stopped at a government building in Sacramento (the state capital) on our way, procuring an apostille stamp for my arduously gathered stack of documents that would be needed to initiate my Israeli naturalization, a process we both approached with some trepidation.

We relished the occasion our honeymoon offered to temporarily slow down the pace of life, intentionally reflect on the whirlwind of the last few months, take leisurely strolls along the rocky beaches, and enjoy a brief respite between the intensity of all things wedding-related and the impending intensity of my international move to Israel and all that it would set into motion.

The week felt like a precious moment in time, during which we ate countless platters of fish and chips, laughed as we discovered a small ice cream shop that sold Dippin' Dots, went whale watching (which made Yonah's mom a little nervous; after all, Yonah is the Hebrew pronunciation of Jonah), strolled through the weekly farmer's market, and hiked the stunning seaside cliffs at Point Lobos State Natural Reserve.

At the end of the week, my parents met us at the San Francisco airport with Dash, my beloved Italian greyhound, who would be coming with us to Israel. "Don't just meet your parents for a few minutes at the airport," a friend had wisely advised. "Be sure you actually build in time to have a meal with them before you part ways." That was the solid and well-intentioned plan, though unexpected traffic and the added uncertainty of where exactly dogs

get ready to board airplanes meant that, in the end, we had exactly
fifteen minutes of rushed hugs and goodbyes with them before we
had to make our way to our gate.

∽·∽·∽

"We ought not therefore to have anything in common with the Jews,
for the Savior has shown us another way," asserted Constantine at
the Council of Nicaea. "It was declared to be particularly unworthy
for this, the holiest of all festivals, to follow the calculation of the
Jews, who had soiled their hands with the most fearful of crimes,
and whose minds were blinded." This moment in the life of the
church is known as the Quartodeciman controversy, as the issue at
hand was the Jewish celebration of Passover on the fourteenth
(*quarta decima* in Latin) day of Nisan.

The Quartodecimans were those who favored reckoning Easter in
accordance with the Jewish community's celebration of Passover.
This was a remarkable position to hold, as it essentially bound the
Christian calendar to the Jewish calendar. Such a linkage became
intolerable for the church as it increasingly sought to untether itself
from Judaism, and the Council of Nicaea solidified this separation.[4]

What was lost in this decision is the intentional connection
made abundantly clear in the Gospels. The meaning and significance of Holy Week can only be understood in full if we have
Israel's history in view as we walk through it. The death and resurrection of Messiah is patterned after the exodus from Egypt, which
serves as the founding event of the Jewish people. As the founding
event of the church, its grafting into Israel's enduring covenant with
God, Jesus becomes the Passover lamb by whose blood the people
of God are spared.

As we've seen in other areas, Christian theology often seeks to
neatly parse out elements that Jewish theology is quite comfortable

leaving in tension. This contrast is likewise highlighted in the eventual distinction between Passover and Easter. For the church, Good Friday is reserved for death, while Sunday is designated as a celebration of resurrection life. This temporal arrangement of worship can end up bifurcating life and death, thus making the bold (and dualistic) statement that, come Sunday, death is no longer a force we need to reckon with at all. We are told to cling to life and to forget the power of death, because Jesus leaves death behind once and for all in his empty tomb. Effectually, the sting of death can be relegated to those outside the church's walls. As we saw with my student Samantha in chapter 6, this message is profoundly disorienting and, ultimately, dehumanizing.

As so many of us have experienced, reality is far different from the simple statement that death has been conquered by resurrection. Death, in all its insidious forms, still pervades our daily lives. Even after Jesus' glorious resurrection, we continue to wrestle with the disquieting dimensions of our humanity: the traumas we relive, the losses we endure, the disappointments we amass, the anxieties we are paralyzed by. And, unfortunately, the church can send the subtle message that to be troubled by these very real struggles is to somehow lack adequate faith or to misunderstand the core of the Christian message.

Passover, on the other hand, embraces the complex intertwining of life and death; in fact, it portrays life and death as convergent, interwoven forces. While life is ultimately triumphant in Israel's narrative, Jewish tradition reminds us that it is impossible to separate the life we experience from our individual and collective memories of death. At the Passover table, we remember the death of a lamb whose flesh and blood spared our lives. We give thanks for the gift of freedom even as our taste buds remind us of the lingering bitterness of slavery. We rejoice in leaving Egypt even as we recall that the Promised Land is still yet not our home. And, remarkably, we intentionally diminish our joy by remembering the suffering of the Egyptians.

Judaism's boldest confrontation with death, however, comes on another day that the Passover story anticipates: Yom Kippur. On Yom Kippur, the Jewish people stand before God in the very throes of death, wearing burial garments, and yet endowed with the courage to believe that God is present and accessible even from the grave. As with Passover, there is no life apart from death on Yom Kippur. Even life, it turns out, does not afford us the ability to forget death. The two stand together in impossible paradox, and we walk out the reality of both as we await final redemption.

Passover and Yom Kippur issue a reminder that we cannot neatly separate or chronologically order life and death. Alas, for now, we must sit in the tension between the two—and this is precisely the place where we encounter the fullness of God's love in Christ, our Passover lamb whose blood atones for sin.

Ironically, the interpretive undercurrents that inform Christian worship on Easter can serve to erase the very context that enables us to fully grasp the meaning of Jesus' death and resurrection. In constructing Judaism as its foil, Christian tradition has all too often obscured the unity and coherence of the biblical narrative, in which God's covenant with Israel is actually the necessary context for the work of Jesus and the founding of the church.

In embracing rather than concealing this tension, we see that Christianity is, albeit often unwittingly, cut from the same cloth as Judaism. Christianity's frayed edges will find wholeness only when they are reconnected with the long-lost threads of the Jewish people.

Seen in this light, the gospel narrative changes from an apparent condemnation of the Jewish people to yet another daring declaration of God's covenantal fidelity to his chosen people. The words

"His blood be on us and on our children!" (Matthew 27:25 TLV) are no longer read as a self-imposed curse, but as an unwitting prophecy of the redemptive power of Jesus' death in relation to his own people. From this angle, Calvary begins to look a lot more like Sinai. The torn veil recalls the broken tablets at Sinai, the death of Jesus invokes the sacrifices of Yom Kippur, the mystery of Holy Saturday mirrors Moses' intercession atop Sinai, and Jesus' resurrection becomes about a covenant renewed once again—a statement of God's endless, unfailing love, first to the Jew, then to the Gentile (Romans 1:16). Approached from this perspective, the joyous declaration that "Christ is risen!" takes on an entirely new depth of meaning. The Savior of the world is, after all, the long-awaited Messiah of Israel.

༄༅༅

The hazy light, the drifts of conversation from fellow travelers, the squiggly Hebrew letters on the signs—it all felt familiar, but also incredibly foreign. As I stepped off the plane in Tel Aviv, I immediately and distinctly felt the difference between Israel being a place I visited and Israel now being my new home. Every time I fly to Israel and watch the little airplane on the TV screen map as it slowly moves along, I'm jarred anew by how close little tiny Israel is to all the big Arab states that so often find their way into the news—Iran, Syria, Saudi Arabia. I took a deep breath and we made our way to the baggage claim.

As we waited for our six suitcases—the entirety of my possessions as I began life in Israel—and Dash (who had been locked in his crate for twenty-four hours of transit), I noticed the woman standing next to me, also waiting for her luggage. She appeared to be in her midsixties and traveling alone. I began to wonder if she was here to visit her daughter (and grandchildren?). How far had she traveled to get here? How did she feel about her daughter living so far away? How long would she be staying for, and how often did she come?

"Let's go, love." Hearing Yonah's voice snapped me out of my daydream and I realized that he had collected all of our luggage. We awkwardly made our way up two escalators and across an outdoor footbridge toward the parking garage. I inhaled deeply, relishing the feeling of outside air in my lungs for the first time since the previous morning. It was night, and my tired eyes created fuzzy halos around the row of streetlights we were passing under. After some Hebrew back and forth between Yonah and the rental car agent, and several attempts to jigsaw my life's possessions into the back of our rented van, Dash curled up on my lap and we began the drive up into the hills of Jerusalem.

11

GOD'S EX-WIFE

For most of the past two millennia, the church's posture toward
the Jewish people has come to expression in the teaching known
as supersessionism, also known as the theology of displacement.

R. KENDALL SOULEN

I t was Thanksgivukkah of my first year living in Israel, a strange
year when Hanukkah (which usually falls sometime in December,
often overlapping with Christmas) coincided with Thanksgiving. I
set off for my morning run, making my way down the hill from our
apartment in the Jerusalem neighborhood of Talbiyeh toward the
walls of the Old City.

I passed First Station, with its quaint shops and charming
sidewalk cafés, crossed the pedestrian bridge over Hebron Road
and descended into the Hinnom Valley (also sometimes translated
Gehenna). From there, I veered onto the narrow trail that snakes
up the hillside and flattens out along the western walls of the Old
City. I ran along the grassy path that hugs the walls, passing the
Tower of David ancient citadel and then Jaffa Gate before curving

left along the outside of the upscale Mamilla mall with its trendy clothing stores and assortment of kosher restaurants, all facing the ancient and history-laden walls.

From there I ran back to our neighborhood on King David Street, passing the Jerusalem YMCA on my right and the historic King David Hotel on my left. Each morning as I ran this same route, I marveled at the fact that I actually lived in Jerusalem. *How did I get here?* I wondered.

Though I could clearly trace each step along the path that led me to this life in this place, and though I never doubted the solidity of the Oslo clarity, everything continued to feel entirely surreal. The desert sandstorms, the intense clip of the Hebrew language, the fact that my new geographical neighbors were now Egypt and Jordan; it was all just *so* foreign.

As Yonah had done for over a decade, I was now living my life in the Jewish homeland, the one place on earth where Jews are a majority of the population rather than a fragment of a per-centage of the population. As I had experienced on my first trip to Israel, the weekly rhythm of Israeli society revolves around Shabbat, and the Jewish holidays buttress the calendar. Though I could taste the richness and textured meaning of these distinct features of life in Israel, they also contributed to my profound sense of disorientation.

For me, the most remarkable part, what made Israel feel like home, was the unity I felt with fellow Jews from all around the world. The lovely French Jewish woman who worked at the corner health food store; the Russian Jews who schlepped on Yonah's moving crew; the sabras who recounted firsthand the Six Day War and every military scuffle since. Somehow, in a world where the Jews are so often the common scapegoat for society's ills, it truly felt as though we were one people.

I had been teaching at Azusa Pacific University since the beginning of my doctoral program, and once I finished my PhD I had also started teaching for Fuller Seminary. I was able to move all of my face-to-face classes online, and the contrast between my Jewish surroundings and my Christian theology syllabi became starker. The posture of Christian theology toward the Jewish people that began with the church fathers, continued through the medieval period and Protestant Reformation, and ran right up into our own day began to feel more personal to me. It was no longer about theological abstractions; now, it was about the people I passed on the streets, bought our weekly produce from, and prayed beside in synagogue.

These people, the Jewish people, *my* people, were the ones who were written out of covenant relationship with God, according to the standard Christian theological narrative. And yet, many of these Jews lived lives of fervent devotion to God, praying each Friday night for God to "accept the prayer of Your nation; strengthen us, purify us . . . turn to Your nation which proclaims Your holiness."[1]

Suddenly, the parting of the ways felt as though it ran through the middle of my very being. I realized that calling into question this troubling and deeply problematic vein of Christian theology needed to be a central task of my teaching and writing.

∽·∽·∽

As we have discussed from different angles, in the centuries after Christ came, Judaism and Christianity increasingly emerge as two mutually exclusive religious traditions. Both traditions develop in ways that intentionally squeeze out Jewish followers of Jesus, who are cast more and more as the excluded middle. Ultimately, Christian theology ends up minimizing God's covenant with the

Jewish people and their ongoing role in the unfolding redemption and consummation of creation.

This well-trod theological trend comes to be known as supersessionism, derived from the word supersede: the Christian community supersedes the role of God's chosen and redeemed people while the people of Israel fade into the background. The most comprehensive treatment of both the history and the theological inadequacies of Christian supersessionism is R. Kendall Soulen's book *The God of Israel and Christian Theology*. In these pages, Soulen examines the deep-seated legacy of Christian supersessionism throughout history and proposes a paradigmatic shift that seeks to overcome this ingrained and destructive framework.

He begins the book with the powerful statement that "the God of Israel is the firm foundation and inescapable predicament of Christian theology."[2] It is the firm foundation because Christian theology crumbles if it is not built on the God of Abraham, Isaac, and Jacob, and it is the inescapable predicament because Christian theology has repeatedly revealed its inability to reckon with the God of Israel's enduring election of the people of Israel.

Soulen introduces the term "canonical narrative," which he defines as an interpretive framework for understanding the story told throughout the Old and New Testaments as a coherent whole. It is not the biblical canon itself, but rather a set of lenses through which Christian theology has historically read and understood the canon. As Soulen describes it, Christianity's canonical narrative is formed around the four movements we discussed in chapter 7: creation, fall, redemption, and new creation.

In Soulen's assessment, "At the deepest level, the problem with the standard canonical narrative is that it makes God's identity as the God of Israel largely indecisive for shaping theological conclusions about God's enduring purposes for creation."[3]

According to Soulen,

> For most of the past two millennia, the church's posture
> toward the Jewish people has come to expression in the
> teaching known as supersessionism, also known as the the-
> ology of displacement. According to this teaching, God
> chose the Jewish people after the fall of Adam in order to
> prepare the world for the coming of Jesus Christ, the Savior.
> After Christ came, however, the special role of the Jewish
> people came to an end and its place was taken by the church,
> the new Israel. The church, unlike the Jewish people, is a
> spiritual community in which the carnal distinction between
> Jew and Gentile is overcome. Accordingly, the church holds
> that the preservation of Jewish identity within the new Israel
> is a matter of theological indifference at best, and a mortal
> sin at worst. Yet the Jews themselves failed to recognize Jesus
> as the promised Messiah and refused to enter into the new
> spiritual Israel. God therefore rejected the Jews and scattered
> them over the earth, where God will preserve them until the
> end of time.[4]

In other words, Christian theology paints Israel as God's ex-wife,
covenantally bound to God and faithful (enough) for a time, but
later cast aside. God then covenants with the church, which becomes God's primary locus for bringing about the fullness and redemption of creation. A central danger of this construal is seldom
recognized by the Christians who either consciously or unconsciously espouse it: If God can so easily annul God's covenant with
Israel, what guarantees God's indefinite faithfulness to the new
covenant people?

In defining Christian supersessionism, Soulen differentiates between three distinct forms: economic supersessionism, whereby

the church replaces Israel not because of Israel's sin but because Israel's role was to prepare the way for spiritual and universal salvation; punitive supersessionism, whereby God abrogates his covenant with Israel on account of Israel's rejection of Christ; and structural supersessionism (which represents the deepest level of supersessionism), according to which Israel (and God's covenant with Israel) is ultimately irrelevant in the overarching narrative of salvation history.

Soulen surveys Christian theology across the centuries, examining the thought of key theological architects (spanning from Justin Martyr in the second century to Karl Barth in the twentieth century) whose work further cements Christian supersessionism. He concludes that Christianity's standard canonical narrative is economically supersessionist, in that it "depicts carnal Israel's role in the economy of redemption as essentially transient by virtue of the spiritualizing and universalizing impetus of God's salvific will," and structurally supersessionist, in that it "renders God's identity as the God of Israel largely indecisive for shaping theological conclusions about how God's works as Consummator and as Redeemer engage creation in universal and enduring ways."[5]

While Soulen's work helpfully diagnoses and describes the problem of Christian supersessionism, and his proposed solution identifies key steps in correcting the problem, at the end of *The God of Israel and Christian Theology* we are left with a new conundrum. In attempting to present a nonsupersessionist account of the narrative unity of the Christian Bible, Soulen ends up unwittingly shrinking the immeasurable significance of Jesus' life, death, and resurrection.

Soulen presents Jesus both as the one who guarantees God's final victory over the powers that threaten creation and the one who points forward toward God's eschatological reign. However, in this volume, Soulen does not address the issue of Christ's divinity, nor does he unambiguously declare Christ's universal applicability and unsurpassibility.[6] In the end, we are left to wrestle with this dilemma and the danger of tipping the balance too far in the other direction.

ഗ•ഗ•ഗ

Now married and living in the same place, Yonah and I began to look toward and imagine our shared future. We were both in our thirties when we met, and he was eager to start a family. This was yet another area where we held different mental timeframes; while I certainly longed to be a mother, I wanted to wait a year after getting married before starting a family to let all the newness set in, improve my embarrassingly basic knowledge of Hebrew, and hopefully have my Israeli citizenship established. After our wedding, I had entered Israel on a three-month tourist visa, and we had not yet begun the process of my naturalization. We had also learned that pregnancy is not covered at all unless one is a citizen, which boded well for convincing Yonah of the soundness of my proposed timeline.

Nonetheless, I apparently needed yet another reminder that life doesn't always conform to our carefully preformulated plans; as it turned out, Yonah won the when-to-have-a-baby debate. On the way home from my Hebrew class one frigid Wednesday night in December, I stopped by a Super-Pharm on Ben Yehuda Street. Having reason to suspect that something had shifted in my body, I grabbed a pregnancy test, sandwiched it between a bar of chocolate and a pair of tights, and presented the bundle to the cashier. I looked away as she scanned the items, quickly paid, and walked home with my heart pounding. I thought for sure I wasn't pregnant; taking a test would ease my mind.

It was a particularly harsh winter in Jerusalem, and Yonah was working late. I felt paralyzed as the test began to display two unmistakable pink lines. I was pregnant. And I began to panic.

I called Yonah, who was just beginning to unload the moving truck on the other side of the city. He was with several workers, who I could hear in the background.

"Ijusttookapregnancytestanditspositive, why aren't you home?!" I screeched hysterically.

"Wow, that's great, mazel tov, I'll be home as soon as I can." We hung up, I crawled into bed and cried myself to sleep.

The two pink lines felt like an assault on the very little bit of control I had left in my life. I had weathered a dizzying amount of change and transition, and I clung to the belief that I would get to decide when to add yet another layer. I was just beginning to find my footing in this new married-and-living-in-Israel season of life, and having a baby felt completely overwhelming.

I was also acutely aware that our baby would be a sabra, and thus would presumably be born with a kind of innate connection to the land and people of Israel that I was only cultivating as an adult. *L'dor v'dor*, "from generation to generation"; perhaps for my child, Jewish identity and faith in Messiah would seem like the most natural combination in the world.

It wasn't long before morning sickness set in, and my days were increasingly spent on our gray IKEA futon. Gazing out the casement windows of our fourth-floor apartment, I perfectly memorized the pattern of barely visible Italian cypress treetops, and the way they swayed in the wind was soothing and hypnotic. I tried (with varying degrees of success) to focus on my work, embrace this new season of life, and not worry too much about the fact that I was now pregnant and not yet a citizen of Israel.

Even amid the insufficiency of Soulen's depiction of Christ, his theology points toward a construal of Israel and the nations that helps overcome Christian supersessionism on account of Christ's work. Soulen sees the "economy of mutual blessing" between Israel and the nations as fundamental to and constitutive of God's work in the world.

This framework allows us to shift the narrative from God's abandoning Israel in order to covenant with the church to God's covenant with Israel *expanding to include the church*. Replacement thus gives way to inclusion. A nonsupersessionist reading of Romans 11 suggests that this is precisely what happens through Christ—the Gentiles are "grafted in" to God's ongoing and enduring covenant with Israel. Rather than the church replacing Israel as the people of God and the bearer of a unique divine commission, Gentile followers of Christ are, in Paul's language, grafted into Israel's mission and redemptive activity.

Soulen is not alone in pointing in this direction; he's joined by a host of post-Holocaust Christian thinkers who envision the relationship between Israel and the church in these terms. Furthermore, as Jewish scholars increasingly reconsider Christianity's central claims, one remarkable development is that even Jewish theologians are beginning to see Christianity in this light.

Franz Rosenzweig prefigures this theological development in the Jewish world. Rosenzweig lived and wrote before the Holocaust, and his thought paved the way for Jewish reflection in subsequent years. In his magnum opus, *The Star of Redemption*, Rosenzweig construes Judaism and Christianity as having complementary vocations, each contributing to redemption and consummation in unique but collaborative ways. Neither is complete without the other, but the distinctiveness of their commissions remains.

The image Rosenzweig offers is that of a celestial star, where the Jewish people represent the inner burning core of the star and Christianity represents the rays of light that emanate outward, bringing the light and heat of the core to the star's surroundings. Judaism, for Rosenzweig, characterizes divine revelation in its purest form, while Christianity effects the proliferation of that revelation. Accordingly, Judaism's central task is to maintain and cultivate its own inner life and connection with God, and Christianity's main task is to bring divine revelation to the ends of the earth.

For Rosenzweig, obedience to the commandments is the means by which the Jewish people lives into its redemptive vocation. Without the Torah, the Jewish people's election is ineffectual and its vocation is unattainable. Rosenzweig thus upholds a strong connection between Israel and Torah, another central connection that Christian reflection often misses. Christianity's vocation, on the other hand, is necessarily missionary—the Christian's task is to bear witness to the revelation of Christ, taking this message to all nations and translating it into all tongues.

The complementary vocations of Judaism and Christianity help the other not to succumb to a set of perpetual dangers and temptations. The physical existence of the Jewish people prevents Christianity from spiritualizing God and fashioning a dualistic notion of covenantal life, and Christianity with its missionary vocation prevents Judaism from retreating into its own cozy covenant with God, disregarding the nations and the invitation they have received to enter into that covenant.

Gentile inclusion in God's covenant with Israel is powerfully illustrated in Ephesians 2:11-22, which unpacks this very concept in a remarkable way. This passage reads,

Therefore, keep in mind that once you—Gentiles in the flesh—were called "uncircumcision" by those called "circumcision" (which is performed on flesh by human hands). At that time you were separate from Messiah, excluded from the commonwealth of Israel and strangers to the covenants of promise, having no hope and without God in the world.

But now in Messiah Yeshua, you who once were far off have been brought near by the blood of the Messiah. For He is our peace, the One who made the two into one and broke down the dividing wall. Within His flesh He made powerless the hostility instigated by the law code of *mitzvot* contained in regulations. He did this in order to create within Himself one new man from the two groups, making peace, and to reconcile both to God in one body through the cross—by which He put the hostility to death. And He came and proclaimed peace to you who were far away and peace to those who were near—for through Him we both have access to the Father by the same Spirit.

So then you are no longer strangers and foreigners, but you are fellow citizens with God's people and members of God's household. You have been built on the foundation made up of the emissaries and prophets, with Messiah Yeshua Himself being the cornerstone. In Him the whole building, being fitted together, is growing into a holy temple for the Lord. In Him, you also are being built together into God's dwelling place in the Spirit.[7]

As one New Testament scholar concludes, "It is the distinctive message of Ephesians that no Gentile can have communion with Christ or with God unless he also has communion with Israel."[8] As in Rosenzweig's star metaphor, the rays cannot exist without the inner burning core of the star. The church's very life is built upon Israel's covenant with God, which Gentiles enter into through the work of Christ and the gift of the Spirit.

⌒·⌒·⌒

As if the disorientation of being a newly-married-now-pregnant-non-citizen-of-Israel wasn't intense enough, the next task was for us to tackle my naturalization. Though I'm fully Jewish, it was as though I had yet to undergo my own personal "grafting in" to the Israeli people. It has become quite difficult for Messianic Jews to be granted Israeli citizenship, as the state considers belief in Jesus to be adherence to a different religion, which nullifies one's claim to the right of return. This practice is inconsistent and discriminatory, and the issue has made its way to the Israeli Supreme Court more than once, yet it endures.

Following our engagement the previous summer, we had consulted with a lawyer who seemed dubious about the prospect of me actually gaining citizenship and who warned us that, should they dig anything up, the state could go after Yonah's citizenship as well. (The lawyer Googled my name during the meeting and laughed out loud as his computer screen displayed the results. "You'll never be able to get citizenship as a Jew," he flatly declared.)

I had arduously amassed a stack of documents to verify my Jewish identity, and on January 23 we presented them at the Ministry of Interior to begin the process of establishing my Israeli citizenship. After twenty-five minutes of waiting in a cramped seating area, surrounded by an impressive cross section of Israel's diverse population, our number was called. We got up, walked to window six and reseated ourselves in the two chairs just opposite a woman who was behind glass and who, from my perspective, held my future in her hands.

In a matter of less than a minute, she thumbed through the thick file I had brought with my carefully arranged documents, chose three single pages to be passed on to the Jewish Agency for thorough vetting, passed the file back to us, and instructed us to schedule a follow-up appointment in six to eight weeks.

On March 22, we anxiously returned to the Ministry of Interior. If all had gone smoothly at the Jewish Agency, we reasoned that this could be the day we would receive news about my successful application for citizenship. If that was not the news that awaited us, we suspected that more trouble and the possibility of a legal battle might lie ahead. Once again, our actual appointment lasted a matter of minutes.

"We have not received your file back from the Jewish Agency," the woman behind the glass flatly reported. "Make another appointment to come back in four weeks."

I had been told that one was not permitted to leave the country for the duration of one's citizenship procurement process, so I quickly and nervously blurted out, after the woman had already called the next number, "I have plans to travel abroad in two weeks . . . will that be a problem?"

"No," she replied. "The airport data system will reflect that your citizenship application is under consideration." I had teaching commitments in the US during the month of April, and I prayed that this woman's casual assurance was indeed accurate.

A few weeks later, I headed to the airport to travel back to the States for the first time since leaving the past fall, which seemed like a lifetime ago. I was looking forward to two weeks of teaching in Colorado, but especially to Yonah joining me in Tahoe to spend time with my family after that.

As it turned out, the airport data system had no record of my pending citizenship application and only reflected my status as having been in the country for the past four months on an expired tourist visa. I summoned my inner Israeli, pleaded with the passport control agent, and after an exceedingly tense fifteen-minute exchange, she reluctantly allowed me to proceed to the gate area. I was immediately flooded with worry about what this might mean for reentry into Israel the following month.

I used the opportunity of being in the States to formally change my last name, and I paid extra to have my new passport rushed so as to be in hand by the time I headed back to Israel. When I went through passport control upon reentry, I presented them with my newly issued passport.

"Is this your first time in Israel?" the passport agent asked as he opened my passport to one of its many completely blank pages.

"No, I've actually been living here but I officially adopted my husband's surname while I was abroad. Would you like to see my old passport?" My chest tightened as I awaited his response.

"No, that won't be necessary. Welcome back to Israel," he replied, stamping my virgin passport and waving me on to baggage claim.

On June 14, Yonah and I returned to the Ministry of Interior. As our number was called, we slowly walked to window four and sat down in ominous silence. The woman behind the glass, who had yet to make eye contact, shuffled through a filing cabinet, placed a number of documents on her desk, made some illegible notes in various places, and slid a single sheet of paper under the glass.

"Sign here to accept your Israeli citizenship," she said.

Yonah and I exchanged a wide-eyed glance. I signed the paper and she directed us up to the third floor. After waiting in another seating area in another large room, our number was called once again. This time, the gentleman behind the glass unceremoniously handed me my *teudat zahut* (Israeli identity card), and my citizenship was final. While I still felt acutely the reality of being the excluded middle, my status as a citizen of the state of Israel made me feel more a part of the Jewish people than I had ever felt before.

Yonah and I celebrated at a nearby bakery, breathlessly recounting the rollercoaster that had begun with the lawyer consultation ten months earlier, and that was now, astonishingly, over. This milestone felt like a significant moment in my own personal mending of the parting of the ways, in my own ongoing struggle to be both a follower of Messiah and a member of the house of Israel, now residing in the homeland of that Messiah and his people.

12

PAUL

With regard to Pauline scholarship it is probably no exaggeration to suggest that Paul's relation to Judaism aptly frames the most important discussions of the twentieth century.

MAGNUS ZETTERHOLM

During the year that Yonah and I dated long distance, I had been invited to Colorado Springs to teach a one-week intensive theology class for Young Life staff members. In the weeks following my intensive course, the director of the program contacted me and asked if I would be willing to teach the class again the following spring.

Though at the time my future was sufficiently uncertain, I began sketching out back-to-back teaching gigs in Colorado that I could commit to, regardless of where in the world I might be residing at that point. Little did I know at the time that I was actually signing up to teach a total of eighty hours in two weeks while being six months pregnant. Ignorance is bliss, as they say.

Morning sickness barely behind me, I boarded a plane back to the States, swelling belly leading the way. After spending a weekend with my parents in California, I headed to Colorado for what would turn out to be both a hugely meaningful mini season of teaching as well as a much-needed time of personal retreat and reflection. My time in Colorado was deeply restorative, reconnecting me with parts of myself that had begun to feel distant and dormant. The long days were full of teaching in actual classrooms with actual students, as opposed to me, myself, and a computer screen.

Each morning, I would walk along Monument Creek on Pikes Peak Greenway Trail, basking in the springtime sunshine and watching the water bubble along over the rocky creek bed. After class, I walked the charming streets of downtown Colorado Springs and daily frequented familiar American restaurants whose otherwise unremarkable fare satisfied my pregnancy cravings and aversions in a way that nothing in the entire city of Jerusalem could. Pregnancy cravings plus culture shock make for an interesting combination, and most of the smells and tastes of Israeli cuisine would rekindle my nausea for many months to come.

As the contours of my course unfolded, the material I was presenting offered an oblique challenge to the way Young Life staffers traditionally preach the gospel, and many of the questions I was asked during the first few days of the course centered on Paul's letters. From the perspective of many of my students, Paul apparently negated the central claims I was making, and which buttressed the entire theological framework I was espousing.

As I gazed out the window of the suite they had given me to stay in for the week (which no doubt usually housed either one large family or about twelve single adults), I knew I needed to scrap my preplanned material for the next day and spend at least a few hours digging into Paul. Exhausted after an entire day of teaching, I opened my laptop and was surprised to discover my second wind as I prepared a completely new outline and PowerPoint presentation.

The next morning, as I walked into the auditorium where our class was being held, an awkward silence washed over the students who had already arrived, their usual preclass chatter suddenly halted. A moment later, I understood. The wit and humor that indelibly characterizes Young Life had struck again; a few students had raided the prop closet, and the taxidermy mountain lion that (oddly?) stood stage right in the auditorium was now adorned with a makeshift tallit and *peyos*.[1] The students weren't sure how I would react to their latest lark. They breathed a collective sigh of relief as they saw a smile spread across my face, joined in with my laughter, and then staged an impromptu photo shoot of big-bellied Professor Jen beside our newly minted Jewish wildlife mascot. I considered it some version of success that these common markers of Jewish identity were now in the vernacular of my Christian students.

〜·〜·〜

The "traditional" reading of Paul has been challenged in recent years, largely prompted by key events of the twentieth century that led Christians to consider anew what our Bibles say about the Jewish people and God's enduring covenant with them.[2] At least since the Protestant Reformation, Paul's letters have offered a natural go-to for enunciating the stark differences between Judaism and Christianity, between "law" and "gospel."

A hundred years ago, it basically went without saying that Paul abandoned Judaism and founded a new religion called Christianity. For much of the history of Christianity since the parting of the ways, a Paul-versus-Judaism framework was essentially assumed. Martin Luther powerfully articulated and contextualized this reading in a way that retained tremendous traction in the subsequent centuries.

In the aftermath of the Holocaust and the founding of the modern state of Israel—events that brought the Jewish people onto the center stage of world history—Pauline scholars began to reassess Paul's position on key theological concepts. One major revision came under the banner of "covenantal nomism," a new category for approaching Paul's view of Torah.

Before we dig into the details of this major revision of Pauline theology and interpretation, we need to understand one key point about language and translation. The word *Torah* in Hebrew means "teaching" and has a fluid array of referents. Most specifically, the Torah is the first five books of our Old Testament, often referred to as the Pentateuch or Books of Moses.

But Torah also has a much larger semantic range; it can mean biblical teaching in general, and in Judaism it also gets applied to the teaching of later rabbinic sages and their interpretation of what it looks like to adhere to biblical commandments. Rabbis' teachings on Shabbat, even today, are often referred to as "words of Torah."

This important note reveals that, in Judaism, the entire history of interpretation of the biblical text informs modern practice. Jewish tradition has long recognized that we cannot straightforwardly live out the commands of the Bible without additional interpretation and application.

For example, what does it mean to "remember the Sabbath day by keeping it holy," as Exodus 20:8 instructs? What does it look like to "make tassels on the corners of your garments," as God commands the Israelites in Numbers 15:38? How does one go about tying these words "as symbols on your hands" and writing them "on the doorframes of your houses," as specified in Deuteronomy 6:8-9?

Judaism's attention to these details reveals a very high regard for Scripture, and for implementing God's directives for holy living. For Jews, these are not questions about meaningless minutia; rather, they form the backbone of faithfulness and obedience to God.

The rabbis and sages shouldered the massive task of arguing and debating about what exactly it looks like to be faithful to God's commandments, providing through their discussions (many of which were later codified in the rabbinic writings, such as the Talmud) a road map for how Jews can faithfully live into the covenant God has made with them.

All of this falls under the umbrella of what Jews mean when they use the word Torah. When the word Torah got translated into Greek (the primary language of the New Testament), it was translated as *nomos*, which means "law." Much of the nuance and richness of what Torah means and signifies was lost in translation, and layer upon layer of negative meaning was gradually piled onto the "law," especially with regard to its fundamental undergirding of Jewish life and faith.

How does all of this relate to Paul? The traditional perspective on Paul assumes that Paul's main grievance against Judaism was its core belief that one earns favor with God by acting rightly, a concept generally referred to as "works righteousness." Judaism was perceived as being all about correct external actions specified in the Torah, while Christianity was understood to be based on faith and grace alone (two of the Reformation's chief slogans). In short, Judaism's core orientation was seen as sharply contrasting with the core claims of Christianity, and Paul championed the latter while dismantling the former.

Scholars of the "new perspective on Paul" (such as E. P. Sanders and James Dunn) began to demonstrate that this is a fundamental misunderstanding of Judaism, including the Second Temple

Judaism of Jesus' day. What they increasingly saw is that the covenant God made with the people of Israel actually has as its basis the exact same foundation as the covenant instituted by Christ.

God forges a covenant with an imperfect, oft-failing people and then, in light of the grace and favor shown to them, calls the covenant people to live in a particular way as God's chosen people. What new perspective scholars realized is that this core sequence applies to both Christianity *and* Judaism's fundamental narratives and self-understandings.

Hence the term "covenantal nomism," which coveys that adherence to the Torah (*nomos*) lives within the bounds of an already established covenantal framework. Human obedience is not the basis of the covenant itself, or of entry into the relationship it establishes. It is also not the most important safeguard of the covenant or the primary means by which it endures. Covenant is established by God as he pursues relationship with his people, who are then called to live lives of obedience in response to their status as the people of God.

What is at issue for Paul, according to the new perspective, is not whether "works of the law" merit God's favor (as in the erroneous "works righteousness" portrayal of Judaism) but the fact that specific Jewish practices serve as a fence between Jews and Gentiles, the former group having always understood itself to be the exclusive people of God.

If Paul imagined a community of Jews and Gentiles together following Jesus—though not in identical ways—then it is of paramount concern that there be no hierarchy or perceived stratification in this twofold community. His admonishments against "works of the law" (as in Galatians 2:16) are not negating Jewish followers of Jesus continuing to live Torah-observant lives, but rather challenging the long-held notion of Jewish particularism, whereby a life of Torah set Jews apart as those who *alone* enjoy covenantal status before God. So, through the lens of the new perspective, Paul's main concern was not denouncing the validity of Torah, but rather emphasizing the unity of Jew and Gentile in Christ.

〜・〜・〜

"Pray for my husband, you guys," I said to my students as I opened our morning class session. As I was eating my way back from the land of culture-shock-meets-morning-sickness, indulging pregnancy cravings to the tune of daily Starbucks lattes and Chipotle salads, Yonah was effectually losing his sanity back on the home front.

In the week that I had been gone, he had started a fire in the toaster, stayed up all night installing makeshift screens in our apartment windows after a plague of mosquitos had descended on Jerusalem, and undertaken the impossible task of decoding the mysterious symbols on our European washing machine, being forced to do laundry for the first time by himself amid his relentless work schedule.

I called him one early afternoon as I sat on a bench in Acacia Park, ice cream in hand. My joyous chirps about how great my time in Colorado was going were met by his middle of the night gruff and grumpy exhaustion. He was retrospectively reconsidering the soundness of this whole plan we had agreed would work out just fine, and he only wanted to discuss how he would absolutely not sign up for this arrangement again. "Okay love, why don't you try to get some rest," I advised, ready to be off the phone and back in my blissful bubble. After all, it was almost time for dinner and I had already planned to once again frequent Poor Richard's, where I had discovered the wonder of jalapeños as a pizza topping.

After I finished my teaching gigs in Colorado, Yonah's bachelor stint happily ended and he flew out to meet me for another two weeks in the States. We spent a weekend babymoon at a historic hotel in Denver and then headed to Lake Tahoe to spend time with my family. We arrived at my parents' house just in time for Mother's Day dinner, which was tender and touching in a whole new way now that I was a mother-to-be.

During our time there, my mom's two best friends threw me the most decadent baby shower in history. I wanted to bottle the richness of it all—the lavish appetizers, homemade desserts, and words of encouragement from those who had known me since my childhood—to take with me back to Israel.

Because of the way our flights were arranged, Yonah flew back to Israel while I headed to Los Angeles for a precious few days of revisiting my former life there. The brimming joy of spending time with my close circle of girlfriends (two of whom were also now pregnant) was the perfect ending to my time in the States. We patronized all of my favorite Pasadena restaurants, laughed over endless amounts of self-serve frozen yogurt, and caught up on months' worth of marriage, career, and morning sickness. While I basked in the sweetness of my former life and my close-knit support network there, I was sharply reminded at every turn that Yonah was not with me and that my home was now with him, in Israel.

I was encountering my own personal kind of "new perspective," not on Paul, but on myself. I realized with poignant force that I could never crawl back into the alluring familiarity of my pre-Yonah life in Pasadena; my center of gravity had shifted, both relationally and geographically. Yonah and I once again were navigating the ten-hour time difference, and as we talked on the phone one morning just before I headed out to breakfast with Amy, he said, "I miss sharing a home with you." I felt exactly the same way.

ↄ·ↄ·ↄ

The so-called new perspective on Paul is actually a multiplicity of new perspectives, all with their unique contours and all of which challenge the traditional Paul-versus-Judaism reading. While the significance of these pioneering scholars cannot be under-estimated, their position now exists as more of a mediating po-sition between the traditional view and an even more radically revised reading of Paul.

While the new perspective scholars challenged the framework that informs the traditional view of Paul, an even newer group of scholars then emerged that pushed these questions and issues even further. Initially referred to as the "radical new perspective" on Paul, this mode of Pauline scholarship is now commonly referred to as the "Paul Within Judaism" school of interpretation. Key scholars in this group include Mark Nanos, Paula Fredriksen, and Anders Runesson.

What these scholars point out is that, even through the lens of the new perspective, Paul is stripped of key Jewish identity markers. Paul is still, in general, negatively disposed toward Torah, and in many cases the term Israel comes to refer to Jews and Gentiles joined together as a kind of "third race."

One of the primary objectives of Paul Within Judaism scholars is to try to reach back into history and read Paul without being influenced by thinkers like Augustine (who definitely formulated the concepts of the fall and original sin) and Luther (who read his own antagonism toward the Catholic Church back into Paul's relationship to Judaism).

To decouple Paul from these later Christian theologians paves the way for reading his letters (and key concepts therein) from an entirely different vantage point. For these scholars, even the notion of Jewish particularism targeted by new perspective scholars betrays the influence of later historical developments. After all, isn't Christianity at least as particularistic as Judaism? According to traditional readings of Paul, doesn't he divide the whole world into those who follow Jesus and those who don't, thus creating a new kind of spiritual hierarchy?

Paul Within Judaism scholars seek to create a conceptual framework whereby Judaism is not construed as the "other" to Christianity (and often the inferior, flawed, imperfect other at that). What if Paul's point was not to highlight Judaism's deficiencies at all? What if he himself lived as a dedicated, Torah-observant Jew until the day he died? What if the main thrust of his writing is to demonstrate the way in which Gentiles are now, through Christ and the gift of the Spirit, being joined together with the people of Israel without becoming Jews?

Reading Paul from this perspective raises a whole new set of questions that must be considered. First, the question of Paul's audience becomes a central point of discussion. Previous generations of Pauline scholarship assumed that Paul was writing his letters to Jews and Gentiles, thus making it difficult to nuance in any way his negative statements with regard to the "law." Paul Within Judaism scholars argue that Paul's audience (in accordance with Acts 18:6 and Galatians 2:9) was *primarily Gentile*. If this is the case, then Paul is merely discouraging Gentiles from believing that they must take on Jewish practice in order to be followers of Jesus. He's fervently trying to convey to them that Christ and the Spirit have made a way for them to be adopted into the people of God *as Gentiles*.

Second, this vein of Pauline scholarship challenges the notion that Paul was Torah observant when he was with Jews and disregarded these practices when he was among Gentiles. If this was the case, it makes Paul's relationship with Torah instrumental rather than intrinsic; it was only in order to "win Jews" that he would maintain Torah observance around them. This position erodes his actual commitment to Jewish practice as a matter of covenant fidelity before God, making it instead merely a matter of missionary expediency. The Paul Within Judaism camp imagines a Paul who was thoroughly and consistently Jewish, committed to Jewish practice in any and all settings.

Third, the Paul Within Judaism framework sharply challenges any notion of Christianity offering a "third race" that is neither Jewish nor Gentile, but a kind of novel category allegedly envisioned in the New Testament. "Third race" theology erases the distinction between Jew and Gentile, positing that the community of Christ followers is primarily defined by the Christian *ethic*, thus relativizing any kind of *ethnic* distinctions. Paul Within Judaism scholars would say that the ethnic distinctions remain, though any hierarchy associated with them is powerfully overcome by the work of Christ and now reflected in the Christ following community.[3]

Fourth, Paul Within Judaism seeks to wrest Paul from the clutches of normative Christian theology and the long, complex road to Christian orthodoxy. This feature naturally goes hand in hand with many of the scholars themselves being Jews, not Christians. The claim is not that Paul Within Judaism is the only objective or unbiased option, but rather that its bias is expressly *not* the concerns of traditional Christian theology.

The entirety of the Pauline corpus looks different from the vantage point of Paul Within Judaism, and this reading has significant implications for contemporary Jewish-Christian relations. As we saw in chapter 2, for Jewish theologian David Novak, Judaism and Christianity are completely mutually exclusive; in his words "the ultimate truth claims of Judaism and Christianity are not only different but mutually exclusive. . . . One cannot live as a Jew and a Christian simultaneously." According to this framework, "The highest form of worship of the Lord God of Israel is *either* by the Torah and the tradition of the Jewish people *or* by Christ and the tradition of the Church."[4] It cannot be both.

Novak's assessment is based largely on the parting of the ways and its aftermath. If we read these developments back into the theology of Paul (as the traditional perspective does), Paul becomes essentially the founder of this mutually exclusive arrangement. He left Judaism behind and embraced Christianity, and his letters leave a record of why and how.

But if Paul never left Judaism behind, if Judaism and Christianity as we now know them didn't even exist as separate traditions until several centuries later, Novak's assertions are called into question. Paul Within Judaism significantly contributes to a widescale reassessment that is taking place in our day between Jews and Christians.

The day I tackled these concepts with my Young Life students was the liveliest day of our entire class. While the students were engaged throughout the course and eager to participate in class discussions, the discussions we had around this material were especially animated, and the students instinctively sensed how much was at stake. It was like I could see the wheels in their brains turning. What does it look like to preach a Christianity that doesn't have Judaism as its necessary foil? Might Judaism actually have something to teach us about Christian discipleship? How do we make sense of the Jewish people's rejection of Christ?

In raising these questions, they voiced some of the most pressing theological issues of our era. Their questions got at the heart of the gospel itself. Rethinking Paul's message causes us to rethink the message that we also proclaim: If Paul wasn't abandoning Judaism for something else entirely, what does this mean for Christian ministry?

ᴄɴ•ᴄɴ•ᴄɴ

I arrived back in Israel just as the heat of summer was setting in. My regular visits to see our midwife became more frequent, and on July 8, 2014 (my mom's birthday), the Israel Defense Forces launched Operation Protective Edge; Israel was now officially at war with Gaza. The escalation in conflict had been triggered by the kidnapping and murder of three Israeli teenagers by Hamas members, and the hazy summer days were punctuated by cascades of indiscriminate rocket fire from Gaza, aimed at Israeli population centers. Israel launched a ground offensive into Gaza with the goal of eliminating Hamas's elaborate tunnel structure that enabled arms and munitions transport from Egypt.

The timing of the war coincided with the most demanding season of Yonah's work that I had yet experienced. Sometimes he would be gone on a job for twenty-four hours and then come home only to eat and take a nap before heading out again. On some occasions, one of their employees would damage an expensive piece of furniture during the move, meaning that Yonah's take-home pay for a grueling job might be next to nothing.

I was coming unraveled, and it felt like all I did was cry. Even when Yonah was home, it was hard to pull myself together, which meant that little opportunities for connection were sabotaged. "Try not to be stressed, Jen; it's not good for the baby." This was the ultimately unhelpful but oft-repeated refrain of a host of well-meaning people. The clarity I had felt in Oslo became blurred, and I daydreamed about the simple riches of my recent trip to the States and the fact that my life there had never included the screeching sound of air raid sirens.

There were four times that summer when the sirens sounded in Jerusalem; each time I happened to be in our apartment, and miraculously, each time Yonah was home. He would hold my hand as I waddled to the stairwell, which functioned as a makeshift bomb shelter, and we would huddle with our neighbors until we heard the BOOM and then return to our apartment.

Amid my overwhelming sense of terror, I developed an intense gratitude for Israel's Iron Dome defense system, which intercepts incoming rockets and detonates them in midair. I marveled at the dizzying realization that someone was crouched at a launch site a mere fifty miles away, intent on killing us. As Jewish Israelis, we constituted the enemy. How was I to navigate life in this country, I wondered, once a tiny human being was entirely dependent on me for its safety and well-being?

One morning in mid-July we sat down with our doula, Amanda, to finalize our birth plan. A high concentration of rockets were raining down on the Rishon Letzion area, which is where our birth was scheduled to take place. "Do you think we need to consider an alternate location?" I asked, realizing that birth and war were equally unfamiliar to me and stumbling over the strangeness and necessity of discussing them together in one conversation. "It would probably be good to develop a plan B," she replied, looking up from the notepad that sat in front of her on our dining room table.

"When is the latest I could fly back to the States?" I asked, bewildered by the thought of potentially giving birth with my family but apart from Yonah, whose work schedule was far too demanding in the summer months to take yet another trip overseas. "You can fly up until you are thirty-six weeks," Amanda assured me, "which means you have until the beginning of August to make that decision."

Amanda had lived in Israel for many years and she knew that it was quite possible there could be a ceasefire in place by then. "You could also go tour Hadassah hospital as an alternate birthing location," she suggested, knowing that a hospital birth was not our desire. "They have a natural birthing center that I think you would really appreciate."

We did end up touring the birth center at Hadassah, and the beginning of August came and went. My toes no longer visible over my ever-swelling belly, I daily reckoned with the fact that the war was dragging on and my window to return to the States had closed.

A lasting ceasefire and fragile truce were signed on August 26, and my contractions began on the evening of August 31. Forty-two hours and two sleepless nights later, our daughter Carmel was born. When we brought her home that night, Yonah's mom was waiting for us at our apartment, tears of joy in her eyes. As I crawled into bed with Carmel on one side of me and Yonah on the other, my heart felt so full I thought it would burst. My abundant life was curled up all around me, in so many ways that I never could have imagined.

This child, born out of our stories, would carry within herself the complexity of both Jewish identity and discipleship to Israel's risen Messiah. Maybe, just maybe, the dark glass that she looks through during her lifetime will have a few less smudges on it than the one we wrestle to see through clearly.

13

A WAY FORWARD

We do not know what to do, but our eyes are turned to You.
Remember, Lord, Your compassion and loving-kindness,
for they are everlasting. May Your loving-kindness, Lord,
be with us, for we have put our hope in You.

Tahanun, Traditional Jewish Morning Prayer Liturgy

Carmel, now fourteen months old, had finally fallen asleep on my once-more swelling belly, and I glanced at my watch. We'd be landing in Los Angeles in a little over two hours, just as the sun's first rays would be flickering over the Pacific Ocean. We were currently flying over Montana, thirteen hours into the fifteen-hour flight and all I could see out the airplane windows was darkness and the occasional faint light in the distance.

After a long series of complicated conversations and decisions, Yonah had left his business in Israel and the future of his career path remained uncertain. We were both looking forward to spending a month with my family in the States, a time to step away from the pressures and uncertainties of life in Israel, a time to rest and reflect.

With no warning, the PA system crackled and an Israeli stewardess announced in an emotionless voice: "We are making an emergency landing due to engine failure. Please fasten your seatbelts." Blunt delivery is part of Israeli culture's unique charm.

As the announcement sunk in, the several hundred mostly Israeli passengers began to rouse from their slumber and a cascade of seatbelt clicks punctuated nervous and choppy conversations. Yonah and I exchanged a pregnant glance, and I watched him quietly pull his pocket siddur out of his backpack and begin praying.

The whole thing felt entirely surreal, and time seemed to warp in an unrecognizable way. My breathing quickened and a thousand thoughts shot through my mind. I tried to remain perfectly still, as if that would somehow steady our apparently failing aircraft.

I'm not sure how long I sat like that, with sleeping Carmel's tiny body slowly rising and falling on top of me; at some point, the flashing lights of emergency vehicles became visible below. There was an audible and collective sigh of relief and a boisterous round of applause as the aircraft's wheels touched the ground. It was still dark outside, and at 4:00 a.m. local time in Billings, Montana, fire trucks escorted our plane to the gate.

I'm quite certain this day was the most exciting day in the career of every Billings airport employee. Two hundred and fifty bedraggled Israelis were deplaned and, for the next eighteen hours, contained within one terminal of the small airport. Billings had no customs facilities, so no one was allowed to leave this designated area. Chabad of Bozeman[1] got wind of our situation and proceeded to deliver enough kosher food to the airport to feed us all for days. We were given pillows and blankets and occasionally updated on our situation.

Finally, at 9:00 p.m., another aircraft arrived that flew us to Los Angeles. The next day, we arrived in Tahoe and moved into my parents' guest bedroom for the next month. I knew that this time in Tahoe would be a significant opportunity to gain new perspective on our lives in Israel. What I did not know at the time was that it would also significantly redirect the coming years of our lives.

∽•∽•∽

The developments in Pauline interpretation that we explored in the last chapter are just one prong of the mutual reevaluation that's taking place in our day between Judaism and Christianity. Indeed, we are living in a remarkable and deeply significant era in this regard.

A number of key events have served as central catalysts for this new chapter in Jewish-Christian relations. First, the Holocaust, which highlighted the ongoing plight of the Jewish people and opened the eyes of many Christians to the dark streak of supersessionism and anti-Judaism that runs through Christian history. Second, and related, the creation of the modern state of Israel and the return of millions of Jews to their biblical homeland. This development seemed more than unlikely (Martin Luther was one of the many to point this out), and Christians couldn't help but raise a new set of theological and exegetical questions in light of this monumental development. Third, new paradigms in biblical interpretation have challenged the regnant view of Judaism and Christianity as two mutually exclusive religious traditions, with Paul serving as the prototypical convert who exposed Judaism's bankruptcy and spent his life touting the riches of its successor, Christianity.

Finally, the emergence of the Messianic Jewish movement in the 1970s has offered a concrete illustration of what it might look like to blur the lines of distinction between Judaism and Christianity and defy the long-held maxim that one cannot be both a Jew and a Christian.

Messianic Judaism has emerged concurrent to a widespread re-evaluation in the world of Christian missions, which is waking up to the fact that the gospel got saddled with Western exports to the rest of the world, bundled together with modern ideals of commerce and culture. As Christian missiologists increasingly see the job of the missionary as supporting people groups around the world in discovering unique expressions of the Christian gospel within their own contexts and cultures (as opposed to replacing those things), Messianic Judaism offers an example of this model in a Jewish context. In the Messianic Jewish movement, the gospel makes a home within the walls of Judaism. Of course, this particular context also happens to be linked to Jesus' own culture and context, and today's living, breathing Jewish people are the heirs of God's covenant with our ancestor, Abraham.

The Second Vatican Council of the Catholic Church, held in the early 1960s, offered the first intentional engagement with the impact of these events on Christian theology. The council issued a document titled *Nostra Aetate* (Latin for "In Our Time") that would, in many ways, set the tone for the coming decades of Jewish-Christian relations. *Nostra Aetate* reflects on God's covenant with the Jewish people, invoking "the bond that spiritually ties the people of the New Covenant to Abraham's stock." Drawing from Paul's olive tree metaphor in Romans 11, *Nostra Aetate* beseeches the Christian church not to forget that it "draws sustenance from the root of that well-cultivated olive tree onto which have been grafted the wild shoots, the Gentiles."

Overturning the historically entrenched Christian trope that the Jews killed Jesus and refocusing on the theological and salvific significance of Christ's death, the document avers that "Christ underwent His passion and death freely, because of the sins of men and out of infinite love, in order that all may reach salvation."

Significantly, the document affirms that, even though "Jerusalem did not recognize the time of her visitation" and many Jews have rejected and even opposed the gospel of Jesus, "God holds the Jews most dear for the sake of their Fathers; He does not repent of the gifts He makes or of the calls He issued—such is the witness of the Apostle." Moving from the theological to the practical, *Nostra Aetate* "decries hatred, persecutions, displays of anti-Semitism, directed against Jews at any time and by anyone."

It is difficult to express how powerful the claims of *Nostra Aetate* are, and the theological yield they deliver. In the face of centuries of Christian anti-Judaism, the document strongly affirms the enduring nature of God's covenant with the Jewish people (contra supersessionism), recognizes the special and unique bond between Jews and Christians, denounces centuries worth of accusations that the Jews killed Christ, and takes a public stand against anti-Semitism in any form. In essence, it positions the Catholic Church—the largest Christian body in the world—as an ally of the Jewish people instead of a rival.

While they have not had the same kind of widespread impact as *Nostra Aetate*, the Protestant Christian world has also issued a number of noteworthy statements regarding the church's fundamental bond with the Jewish people.[2] In short, *Nostra Aetate* set into motion a widespread Christian reappraisal of the Jewish people and the relationship between Judaism and Christianity, a sweeping ecclesial movement whose implications continue to ripple outward.

ᔕ•ᔕ•ᔕ

It was about one week into our visit that the reality struck me in a blinding sort of way. I nursed the staggering realization internally for a few days before calling Roz, who continued to be a cherished friend and mentor. I felt disoriented, unsure, and bewildered.

"Roz, I cannot return to Israel next month," I verbalized for the first time, bluntly. This conclusion had become increasingly clear to me over the course of our time in Tahoe, but I hadn't yet spoken it out loud.

For me, having Carmel had changed everything. It changed me. Living ten thousand miles away from my family and seeing them twice a year had become almost unbearable.

Added to this was the reality that we were living through a particularly violent time in Israel. The Gaza war just before Carmel's birth gave way to a series of car rammings across the city of Jerusalem (one of which claimed the life of a two-month old baby girl one mile from our apartment when Carmel was two months old), which gave way to the "knife intifada"[3] (several months of terrorism in the form of brutal stabbings—at the height, about three per day—at indiscriminate locations all across the country).

I became fearful of leaving our apartment and I longed for life in the US with every fiber of my being. In an attempt to maintain some kind of grounding normalcy, I would force myself to take a thirty-minute walk with Carmel every day and I would count down the minutes until we could return home, my heart racing with each person who passed us along the way. At night, I could only sleep if I was touching Carmel, feeling her breathing. Any luster that Israel had once held was completely obscured. I felt as though I was sinking. To top it all off, our second child would be arriving in four months and Yonah had no job to return to in Israel.

I breathed a bit easier as I listened to Roz affirm my utterly unexpected and almost incomprehensible declaration. "Jen, there's no way you can go back like this. You need a break."

The next task was to broach the topic with Yonah and set into motion a drastic change of course for our lives. Yonah's lifelong dream was to be in Israel, a dream he had been living out for over a decade. For him, as the Jewish homeland, Israel was home. Its theological significance informed his very being, and his commitment to living there significantly shaped his life's goals and priorities.

What I agonized over during our dating relationship was that, in marrying him, I would be signing on to this vision for our lives, joining him in something that felt much less familiar and ideologically engrained in me but that would nonetheless characterize our future together. Even the Oslo clarity I had received had included living in Israel, which I understood to be part and parcel of choosing a life with Yonah.

Now it was as though I was going back on all of that, refusing to proceed in the direction we had agreed on, singlehandedly steering our futures in a radically different way. While I latently felt the impending weight of it all, I also felt a small, quiet inkling that perhaps this unexpected change of course was not merely the assertion of my wayward will; perhaps it was, in some inscrutable way, God's working.

At the time, for Yonah, this seemed like an impossibility. From his perspective, God had led him to Israel, I had signed on to this vision, and I was now disrupting the building blocks of both his carefully shaped identity and the future hope of our children sharing in that identity.

And yet, amid an unspeakable amount of grief and disorientation, Yonah's love for me and his commitment to our family prevailed. The rest of our trip was spent delving into the logistics of yet another international move, this time abrupt and unexpected. Then, in the midst of a swirling snowstorm, Yonah boarded our scheduled return flight alone. He spent a whirlwind two weeks in

Israel, packing up our lives and preparing to start an entirely new life back in the States.

During his time in Israel, two things happened that seemed like small yet significant reminders that God was there, with him in the anguish and bewilderment, promising to still guide our lives even outside the Promised Land. First, our beloved friend Baruch (who had been instrumental in setting us up) spoke the words of Jeremiah 29:7 over Yonah: "Seek the peace and prosperity of the city to which I have carried you into exile. Pray to the LORD for it, because if it prospers, you too will prosper."

These words, spoken by the prophet Jeremiah to the exiles in Babylon after the devastating destruction of the first Jerusalem temple and forced deportation of the elite class of Jewish priests and prophets, came as a ray of hope in one of the darkest hours in Jewish history. Uprooted from their land, no longer able to worship in their now razed temple, the exiles no doubt wondered if God had forsaken them. Amid their confusion and despair, God commissioned them to dedicate themselves to investing in the welfare of Babylon, the last place they wanted to be. This notion would become a guiding principle for Yonah during his own unwitting experience of exile.

Second, Yonah heard a rabbi preach at a Shabbat service that struck him profoundly and again seemed to speak directly into his current situation. The message was focused on Jacob, and the rabbi explained how, when Jacob returned to Bethel in Genesis 35, perhaps he interpreted his own travails as the fulfillment of God's prophecy to Abraham in Genesis 15:13 that his descendants would struggle in a country not their own. However, as Jacob would later learn through the saga with his son Joseph, the true exile had not yet begun—and God had in store an even greater deliverance than what Jacob had ever imagined. Yonah, about to begin his own sojourn in a foreign land, an Egypt of sorts, found comfort in this reminder that the Israelites' presence in Egypt was the very occasion that led to the exodus, God's paradigmatic rescuing of his people.

And so, on New Year's Eve, laden with a decade's worth of memories, two poignant mental reminders of God's work in the midst of exile, and a crated Dash, Yonah boarded a plane back to the States.

ᔕ•ᔕ•ᔕ

The Second Vatican Council set into motion a widespread Christian reevaluation of Judaism and the Jewish people, which has been met by a reciprocal reappraisal of Christianity by many leading Jewish rabbis and organizations. "These developments represent a new kind of Jewish-Christian encounter, made possible by Christians increasingly recognizing and renouncing the supersessionism that has plagued Christian history, and Jews increasingly acknowledging that Christian theology is not inherently anti-Jewish."[4]

While it is now quite common for Jews and Christians to collaborate on all kinds of initiatives, the theological aspect of the remarkable era in which we're living is especially striking. There are four key markers of this new Jewish-Christian encounter.

First, the Jews and Christians engaged in this stream of dialogue are unabashedly committed to their respective traditions, and they view their religious particularity as an asset rather than a liability in their interfaith work. In other words, it is as committed Christians and committed Jews that they seek to engage with and better understand the other; their religious commitments are not separate from or ancillary to their engagement with one another.

Second, these scholars are attempting to understand the religious tradition of the other in the terms and categories of their own religion. This approach enables rich theological exchange, for the religious particularity of the other is engaged in relation to (rather than in isolation from) one's own deeply held convictions. This trend goes against the ingrained paradigm of Christianity and Judaism being conceived of as mutually exclusive religious traditions, with incompatible core claims and divergent theological orientations.

Third, the theologians representing the new Jewish-Christian encounter perceive a deep underlying commonality between Judaism and Christianity. While they do not minimize or ignore the significant theological and historical differences between these two religious communities, they recognize that the bond between these two entities is nonanalogous to any other pair of religious traditions. In short, they recognize that each community and tradition cannot be accurately understood or described without reference to the other.

Finally, and perhaps most significantly, these theologians are beginning to reconceive their own religious identity and self-understanding in light of their encounter with one another. If Judaism and Christianity are mysteriously and indelibly bound together, then it follows that they can only properly be defined with reference to one another.

This sort of posture opens up entire new vistas of possibility with regard to Jewish-Christian relations, and it offers a promising framework through which to challenge and rewrite the dominant paradigm of mutual exclusivity and hostility toward one another that has historically characterized the relationship between Judaism and Christianity.

If, as Pope John Paul II contends, Judaism is somehow "intrinsic" to Christianity, then the full implications of the new Jewish-Christian encounter on Christian theology are only beginning to become clear. Ultimately, if the enduring and thoroughgoing connection between Jews and Christians is real, it must work its way through every doctrine of Christian theology. It cannot be isolated merely to Christian views on evangelism or ecclesiology; it must inform each and every Christian doctrine. In other words, its effect on Christian self-understanding must be total . . . In sum, if Judaism is intrinsic to Christianity, then *no doctrine of Christian theology can be understood without reference to Judaism and the Jewish people.*[5]

The burgeoning of this new relationship holds great promise for healing, reconciliation, and redemptive partnership, and its full impact is still being played out. While we cannot be sure where this new trajectory will lead, we can stand in awe at the tumultuous path that has led us here, and the invitation we've received to participate in its remarkable contours.

The momentous developments regarding the relationship between Judaism and Christianity also have significant implications for the Messianic Jewish movement, and the in-between existence of Jewish followers of Jesus. While history has designated this group as the "excluded middle," many scholars and theologians today are beginning to see Messianic Jews as an essential link between the church and the Jewish people, reclaiming an understanding closer to what we see represented in the New Testament. Messianic Jews connect Christians to the wider body of Israel, the strong and steadfast root into which they have been grafted. After all, if the church is to truly understand its own identity, it must understand the covenant body to which, through Christ, it has been joined together.

This is why, when I teach about these developments, I begin with Judaism's *shechecheyanu* prayer: "*Baruch atah Adonai Eloheinu melech haolam, shehecheyanu, v'kiy'manu, v'higiyanu laz'man hazeh.*"

(Blessed are You, Lord our God, King of the Universe, who has kept us alive, sustained us, and brought us to this season.)

ᘓ·ᘓ·ᘓ

There are two main words that refer to the Jewish people's existence outside the land of Israel. The first word is *galut*, a Hebrew word that literally means exile and conveys the political and emotional duress of a people uprooted from its land and subject to alien rule. Technically, this term and the reality it represents came to an end once the modern state of Israel was founded and it once again became possible for the Jewish people to live sovereignly in their homeland.

The second word is *diaspora*, a Greek word meaning dispersed or scattered and typically referring to the more neutral reality that nearly half of the world's Jewish population continues to live outside the land of Israel, even after the founding of the modern state of Israel in 1948.

For Yonah, in the company of many other Zionist Jews, the term *galut* still applies; for him, our lives in Tahoe are experienced as a kind of exile that he willingly accepts because his commitment to us, his nuclear family, trumps his ideological commitment to living in Israel. That he daily seeks the welfare of our current city and rarely verbalizes his lament at having left Israel is a testimony to both the strength of his character and his deep-seated belief that God indeed continues to guide and anchor our lives, wherever we are.

Three months after Yonah rejoined us in the States after wrapping up our lives in Israel, our son Asher was born. His birth was beautiful and redemptive, and he has lived up to the meaning of his name—happy or blessed—bringing immeasurable joy and laughter into our home. His middle name is Israel, lest our son born in *galut* forget where the true home of our people is.

According to Franz Rosenzweig, a Jewish person's identity is like "an inner home that he may as little get rid of as the snail its house, or to use a better metaphor: a magic circle from which he can as little escape as can his blood from circulation, just because, like and with this latter, he carries it everywhere he may ever walk or stand."[6] As we continue to make our home in Tahoe, ten thousand miles from the covenantal home of the Jewish people, our identity endures. I'm reminded of this reality each Friday night as I watch Yonah lay his hands on each of our children's heads and bless them with the Aaronic Blessing. I'm reminded of it each and every day as the rhythms of our lives are etched by the countercultural contours of the Jewish calendar. I'm reminded of it as our children study Hebrew alongside English, sometimes excelling in the former more than the latter.

While the details of my inability to return to Israel and the series of events it set into play remain complex, our lives are now based in my hometown, a place I thought I would never again live.

Our house is around the corner from my parents' house, the house I grew up in, and relationship with my parents is a cornerstone of my children's lives in a way I never could have imagined. FaceTime calls between Carmel and my parents during our time in Israel have now given way to my children and my parents living life together on a daily basis. Having not lived in Tahoe since graduating from high school over twenty years ago, my life here continues to both delight me with its sweetness and bewilder me with its unexpectedness.

As I sit here tapping away on the keys of my laptop, I hear drifts of laughter coming from upstairs where my kids are with my mom, reading books and eating snacks. The rhythm of our life is precious and predictable, in a way and in a place I never imagined. The very streets where I used to ride my bike as a child are where I'm now teaching my kids to ride their first bikes. Somehow, just as when I was a kid, this is home. While our most abundant lives may yet still be in Israel, what these years in Tahoe continue to reveal is that this too was always part of my dream (and God's dream for us?), albeit dormant and unrecognized for many years.

Our current residence in the States lends a certain symmetry to our marriage, for each of us now knows what it's like to sacrifice so very much to be together. This season has been full of restoration for me, a time to reclaim so many things lost or given up along the way; in an odd and uncanny way, for Yonah, it is a season of losing those very things.

The communities that ground us represent both the fragmented nature of our religious identities and our commitment to forging bridges and imagining new pathways forward. We are deeply involved with the local Jewish community as well as a local evangelical church, and we visit the nearest Messianic Jewish synagogue (which is two hours away) as often as possible. Somehow, this patchwork of community matches the patchwork of our own identities, and the fact that we find rich sustenance in each while not entirely fitting into any of them seems significant.

For me, the community I feel most at home in is Yachad BeYeshua, and its global, diffuse, and ecumenical nature paradoxically helps me to hold together the various pieces that make up an increasingly composite yet rewarding version of myself. In our little corner of the world, we are seeking to live out a vision of Judaism and Christianity where each tradition is enriched by the other, and where passageways back and forth become increasingly well-trod.

If this is our exile of sorts, it remains true that God has always used times of exile to shape his people. After all, it was in Babylon, the place of Israel's apparent godforsakenness, that the great tomes of the Talmud were produced, the pages of which continue to guide the life and practice of the Jewish people around the world to this day. As God speaks through the prophet Hosea, God leads his people into the wilderness in order to speak tenderly to them (Hosea 2:14).

Indeed, exile is a time of shaping, of refining, of God increasingly molding his people for his purposes. These themes very much ring true for our own experience of being back in the States. In many ways, it has been a time of healing, a time of both profound rest and profound productivity. So often, the way forward feels like a step backward, and the biblical narrative affirms that that life of God's people is anything but linear.

And yet, as the arc of the biblical narrative reveals, the exile will come to an end. A mere handful of verses after Jeremiah exhorts the exiles to "build houses and settle down" in the land of their exile, God promises that they will be brought back to the Promised Land, that their time of exile will come to an end, just as the Israelites' time in Egypt came to an end.

We too are living in this in-between time, enjoying the rich harvest of our lives in California yet poised for God, in his timing, to bring us back to the Promised Land. My hope is that we will be stronger, more faithful, more joyful, and more hopeful for our time spent in Tahoe, however long it may last. Though the way forward is uncertain, my prayer is that God would use this time to shape us more into the people he has created us to be, that he will cultivate in us a deeper sense of his abiding presence—and the ability to recognize that it makes all the difference in the world.

EPILOGUE

The Jewish Gospel

When I first became a follower of Jesus in college, my Jewish identity seemed irrelevant. So I set it aside and sought to be a Christian in the way that my closest friends were. As I look back, I feel especially grateful for the few friends who wouldn't quite let me forget my Jewishness.

Like Kelly, who lived next door to me in the freshman dorms and quickly became one of my closest friends. "Jen, you're part of God's chosen people, the 144,000!" she reminded me, more than once. At the time, this meant nothing to me, other than it being something that made me different from my Christian friends, which was the last thing I wanted.

And Mikayla, who would leave me voicemails and send me cards on Jewish holidays long before those holidays meant much to me. She had studied with Marvin Wilson at Gordon College and developed a deep love for all things Jewish, including me and my family. "Happy Simchat Torah!" her message would begin.

For me, these gestures on the part of my friends seemed somehow out of place, even unwelcome. They felt like disruptions to the person I was becoming and wanted to be. *Sure, I was raised in a Jewish family,* I thought, *but now I am a follower of Jesus.*

As it turns out, however, these reminders issued by my Christian friends were the steppingstones that would ultimately lead to my realization (and eventual embrace) of a core tension within my identity. And that tension would in turn fuel my life's greatest passions.

It would take a few years for the nagging sensation that I had left a fundamental piece of myself behind to surface. But once it had, there was no going back.

I sometimes wonder, *Might it have been simpler to just let sleeping dogs lie, to let the Jewish part of myself fade into the background? To simply self-identify as a Christian, like over two billion people in the world do?*

In one sense, yes. It's always simpler to fit into neat and well-established boxes. But I believe that my life would have been robbed of much of its richness had I chosen this path (or, perhaps more aptly, had it chosen me). The path I have found myself on instead, fraught with uncertainty and in-betweenness, has turned out to be the font of my life's great joy. It is this path, with all of its toil and misunderstanding, tears and anguish, that has proven to be my meeting place with God—the God of my ancestors, the God of Israel, the God who is fully revealed in the person of Jesus Christ.

But let me assure you, it has been far from one continuous mountaintop experience. My journey has been full of fear, doubt, and a great deal of loneliness. In an uncanny way, it is precisely these aspects of my experience that have opened my eyes to the precious gifts and guides that God has sent along the way. Events like my Birthright trip, during which I would stumble upon yet another layer of my complex identity. People like Mark Kinzer, who assured me early on that though I may be lonely, I am not alone.

When offering guidance on how to engage in healthy theological discussion, my friend and colleague David Rudolph encourages us to *follow the disturbance.*[1] When we feel pricked by a concept or claim that presents a challenge to our worldview, goading us to push back, do we feel comfortable sitting in this place just a bit longer before our innate response kicks in? Are we able to tolerate the cognitive dissonance, or do we instinctively retreat into the cozy cavern of complete resolution?

Oftentimes when I teach Christian theology, I have my students write the gospel—the good news about Jesus Christ—in one sentence.[2] Then we have a discussion about what they have written: What portion of Scripture did each student focus on? What did Jesus primarily come to do and bring? Did Israel get mentioned?

My goal in this exercise is to challenge my students to see the gospel as representing a pivotal chapter in a story that began long before Jesus came onto the scene, rather than something that appears out of nowhere and whose key terms acquire meaning out of thin air. In reality, the anchoring vocabulary of Christianity is rooted in the language of Israel's Scriptures, and words like God, Messiah, blessing, prayer, praise, thanksgiving, salvation, and redemption only make sense by referring to the story told in those Scriptures.[3] *If the gospel we preach has nothing to do with God's covenant with Israel, I believe we have missed something profound.*

This claim may be disconcerting, and rethinking the gospel in this light might require quite a bit of reconceptualizing categories and conclusions. In the end, it can be unsettling to have a concept so fundamental to the New Testament and subsequent Christian faith challenged. The important question is, What do we do with this sense of unsettledness? Does it cause us to plug our ears and withdraw into the land of familiar concepts and well-trod ideas? Or can we approach our unease with a sense of curiosity, a willingness to follow the thread and see where it may lead?

My therapist often mentions the way in which family systems are like a thermostat. The default is to stay at a certain temperature, employing a go-to way of operating, and any kind of disruption is met with fierce pushback. "Nope, we're staying at 68 degrees," the system responds. We may conclude that the thermostat is right, that trying to adjust the temperature is a waste of time or too risky. But we may be wrong.

One of my goals in this book has been to lay bare a very powerful theological thermostat. Christian history has been holding on to a default narrative that resists being challenged, that clings to certain biblical passages and historical figures that reinforce the dominant narrative.

Yet, we are living in an era in which key Christian theological categories are increasingly being rethought, and a central aspect of this rethinking has to do with the relationship between Judaism and Christianity, Israel and the church.

If I had to summarize the aim of this book in one sentence, it would be to bring this theological phenomenon onto the radar screen of passionate Christians, and thereby to raise questions about the very gospel we preach. My goal is to retrace the history that ultimately declared Judaism and Christianity to be two separate (and largely incompatible) religious traditions and to challenge the conclusions that are often drawn as a result of that history.

My hope is that, as you finish this book, you feel slightly troubled. Troubled by the way that Christian faith tends to operate just fine with little or no mention of the people of Israel and God's covenant with them. Troubled by the supersessionist sermons you've heard over the years. Troubled by the way in which "those legalistic Pharisees" are always cast as the bad guys in Christian theology.

I hope you walk away from this book not with pat answers to difficult theological issues, but with a *new set of questions* to ruminate on and sit with. Questions about the fundamental and indelible connection between the Christian church and the Jewish people, and what this might mean for you and your community. Questions that might on occasion keep you up at night, questions that you will raise in your weekly Bible study or on the phone with a friend.

My hope is that you'll follow the disturbance and see where it leads. That you will embrace the tensions you feel, even without a clear sense of how or if they will ever be resolved. And finally, my hope is that these tensions may indeed lead you into a deeper and richer life of faith and discipleship in which you find yourself loved and embraced by Israel's great God.

ACKNOWLEDGMENTS

In my experience, writing a book is like taking a journey, and I am so thankful to have had such a wonderful group of companions on this particular book journey.

I'm thankful for my many students over the years, who have offered me a wonderful forum to float many of the ideas and arguments presented in this book. Thank you for your feedback, your engagement, and your willingness to entertain new and sometimes challenging ideas.

Thank you to Katelyn Beaty, who helped cast a vision for this book in its current form.

I don't think this book would have ever seen the light of day without the incredible guidance of my agent, Keely Boeving, who also served as a treasured reader along the way. Thank you for championing this project, Keely!

Many thanks to my other five readers as well: Claire Crisp, Mark Kinzer, Andie Cohn, Michael Stone, and Amy-Jill Levine. Your input along the way has been absolutely invaluable, and the book is much stronger for your careful feedback on each chapter. Special thanks to Michael Stone for his meaningful collaboration on chapter 10 and Matt Thiessen for his input on chapter 4.

I'm also extremely grateful for the team at IVP and in particular my editor, Al Hsu, who gained a vision for the project early on and has been incredibly supportive, responsive, and diligent throughout the writing and revision process. If there's a world record for number of emails written by an author to an editor, I think I might have broken it.

Thank you to Deborah Edgar, who helped me maintain some semblance of sanity throughout the Covid-19 pandemic as I wrote this book.

I am profoundly grateful for the daily support of my husband, Yonah, my anchor, my home, the one who enables me to thrive in so many significant ways that I all too often take for granted. And to my kids, Carmel and Asher, who model for me on a regular basis what patience and kindness look like.

And finally, a huge thank you to my parents for the incredible ways they support our family and my professional ventures each and every day. Mom and Dad, this book is dedicated to you and would not have come to be without you. You are truly an inspiration.

QUESTIONS FOR REFLECTION OR DISCUSSION

INTRODUCTION: ON BEING MONSTROUS

1. What drew you to your current church or community? What aspects of your community continue to be the most meaningful for you?

2. In your church context, how is Judaism generally portrayed? What about the Jewish people? Are there specific references that stand out to you?

3. What interaction have you had with Jews? What has been the main context (friends, family members, coworkers, etc.) and tone (combative, friendly, surface-level, etc.) of these interactions?

1. THE PARTING OF THE WAYS

1. Who have been significant mentors in your life, and how have they helped to shape your self-understanding?

2. In your church context, is the Nicene Creed recited? What does this creed, or other historical Christian creeds, mean to you?

3. What is your response to the seventh-century conversion liturgy quoted? In your experience (or from your perspective), what becomes of Jews who come to faith in Jesus?

2. The Excluded Middle

1. When is a time when you didn't fit in? How did you respond?

2. Jewish theologian David Novak claims that "the ultimate truth claims of Judaism and Christianity are not only different but mutually exclusive. . . . One cannot live as a Jew and a Christian simultaneously." Do you agree? What are the implications of his claim, whether or not one endorses this perspective?

3. How do you respond to the statement that "Jews *as Jews* and Gentiles *as Gentiles* now together form the community of Messiah"? What might it mean for Jews and Gentiles to follow Jesus in different ways?

3. Lost in Translation

1. What experiences have been most formative for you in your own process of self-discovery, religious or otherwise? What made them so meaningful?

2. In your religious circles, how are Old Testament commandments generally interpreted and understood? Are they seen to have any kind of ongoing meaning or significance?

3. How do you approach Paul's "grafting in" metaphor? From your point of view, what is going on in this metaphor between the Christian community and the people of Israel? What is at stake in our understanding of this passage?

4. Jesus and Ritual Purity

1. What are some of your favorite books, and why were they so meaningful for you?

2. What would you describe as "forces of death" in our culture and context? What does it look like to oppose them?

3. Does a deeper understanding of Jesus' relationship to the Old Testament ritual purity system affect your understanding of the gospel? If so, how?

5. "The Land I Will Show You"

1. Have there been times in your life when you have heard clearly from God? What were the circumstances and what was it like for you?

2. How do you relate to the centrality of the land of Israel in Jewish life and thought? What do you think the implications are of Judaism being a "landed" religion?

3. How do the political issues surrounding the modern state of Israel affect your understanding of the role of the land in the Bible?

6. Bodies

1. For you, what are some of the most powerful spiritual practices? How do they engage the body, and why do you find them meaningful?

2. Do you notice traces of dualism in your own faith or spirituality? Has dualism colored the way you read the Bible and understand the gospel?

3. What is most challenging for you in terms of embracing embodied existence? What do we gain by doing so, and what are the risks?

7. Sin and the Fall

1. What core tensions exist in your life? How do you respond to them, and what does this look like?

2. How do you, or the community you're a part of, understand the fall? What role does it play in your understanding of the Bible?

3. What do you make of the claim in Judaism that obedience to the commands of God is possible? What are the implications of this claim?

8. Sabbath

1. Do you keep any kind of sabbath? What does this concept look like for you and what does it mean to you?

2. For you, does too much silence or stillness lead to anxious restlessness? If so, how do you tend to respond to this?

3. Why do you think God rested on the seventh day, and what might this mean for Christians?

9. The Spirit

1. How to you tend to think about freedom? How does the notion of freedom inform your faith?

2. What do you make of the claim that the coming of the Spirit means something different for Jews than for Gentiles?

3. What do you see as the significance of the connection between Shavuot and Pentecost?

10. Sacred Days

1. What are the most "sacred days" in your own life and spirituality? What do these days look like and mean for you?

2. Does your celebration of Easter include any mention of Passover? In your community, what (if anything) does the connection between the two holidays mean?

3. How do death and life continue to coexist in our world today, and how are we to interact with and respond to the presence of both?

11. God's Ex-Wife

1. Have you had any experiences of deep disorientation or culture shock? What did they feel like, and how did you navigate them?

2. From your perspective, what becomes of God's covenant with the people of Israel once Jesus comes?

3. How have you generally understood Ephesians 2:11-22? Does the discussion of Christian supersessionism and God's expanded covenant with Israel shift your perspective on this passage?

12. Paul

1. When was a time when your perspective on something underwent a major shift? How did you experience the process, and what was at stake?

2. Has your understanding of Paul been informed by the traditional reading, exemplified in Luther's thought? If so, what has this meant for your personal theology?

3. What Pauline passages are most difficult to reconcile with a Paul Within Judaism perspective? Which passages clearly support it?

13. A Way Forward

1. What does home mean to you? Is it a place, or a set of memories and experiences, or a concept whose meaning changes based on your circumstances?

2. What experiences have you had of collaboration between Christians and Jews? Do you feel any kind of pull toward deliberate engagement with the Jewish people?

3. What are your three main takeaways from this book? Has any aspect of your personal theology been challenged, or affirmed, or enhanced?

GLOSSARY OF JEWISH
AND HEBREW TERMS

aliyah: (Literally, "ascent") The return of Jews to their ancestral home, the land of Israel. This is understood to be an "ascent," as the land of Israel is on a higher spiritual level than the lands of the diaspora. There have been Jews returning to Israel since the exile in the first century, but in the modern period we see specific waves or movements of Zionist aliyah beginning in 1882.

Amidah: (Literally, "standing") Also called *Shmona Esreh*, it is the other central Jewish prayer, together with the *Shema*. The *Amidah* is recited three times on weekdays and consists of nineteen blessings, prayed silently, while standing and facing Jerusalem.

Birkat Hamazon: Prayers said after eating a meal, based on Deuteronomy 8:10. The prayers include thanks to God for the food, for the land of Israel, for building the city of Jerusalem and for God's goodness.

challah: The name comes from the proscribed offering of a portion of any dough to the priest in temple times (Numbers 15:18-20). Today it tends to refer to bread baked specially for Shabbat. There are many different kinds of challah, including the sweet, braided bread that originated among Jews of Eastern European origin. Shabbat meals require two loaves of bread, commemorating the double portion of manna that fell before Shabbat in the desert (Exodus 16:22-27).

chametz: Leavened grain products. It is forbidden for Jews to eat, own, or benefit from *chametz* during the seven days of Passover (eight days outside of Israel). Thus, a big part of preparing for Passover is searching for and getting rid of the *chametz* in one's home and possession.

chuppah: The wedding canopy under which a Jewish couple is married. It can be made of any kind of cloth and is held up with four poles, one in each corner. The *chuppah* symbolizes the Jewish home that the couple will build together. In traditional Judaism the wedding ceremony is held outside so that above the *chuppah* is only sky.

diaspora: A Greek word meaning "scattered" or "dispersed," which has come to refer to the Jews who live outside the land of Israel. See also *galut.*

galut: (Pronounced *golus* in Yiddish) The exile and scattering of the Jewish people from their homeland in the land of Israel, out into diaspora among other nations of the world. Today the Jewish people are about equally divided in number between those who live in Israel and those who live in the diaspora.

Hamotzi: (Literally, "who brings forth") A way to refer to the blessing made before eating bread, whose words are "Blessed are You, Lord our God, King of the Universe, who brings forth bread from the earth."

Hanukkah: An extrabiblical festival that celebrates the rededication of the temple after its liberation from the Seleucids under Antiochus IV Epiphanes in the second century BC. The festival falls in the winter, on the 25th of the Hebrew month of Kislev, and lasts for eight days. It is celebrated by lighting an additional candle each day until eight lights are burning, the eating of oil-fried foods and spinning of special four-sided tops called *dreidels.* While a relatively minor holiday, it receives a lot of attention especially in the West due to its seasonal proximity to Christmas.

Havdalah: (Literally, "separation") A short prayer said at the end of the Sabbath on Saturday night. Using wine, spices, and fire, the prayer serves to distinguish the Sabbath from the rest of the week.

kashrut: (Literally, "fit" in the sense of "acceptable" or "proper") Dietary laws followed by observant Jews. These include permitted or forbidden foods as well as laws for the correct preparation and consumption of permitted foods.

kippah: A small round head covering worn by traditional Jewish men at all times, and by more liberal Jews only when in synagogue. It is considered a sign of reverence for God, remembering that God is above us. Also sometimes called a *yarmulke.*

kittel: A simple white garment that serves as a burial shroud and is also worn by some men traditionally on *Yom Kippur* and when leading a *Pesach seder.* It is also traditionally worn by a groom at his wedding ceremony, symbolizing purity.

midrash: A classical form of Jewish biblical interpretation that seeks a deeper meaning beyond the literal text by attending to language, using allegories, and filling in textual gaps.

minyan: The smallest number of Jews required to constitute an acceptable quorum for community prayer. According to traditional Judaism only adult Jewish men (over the age of 13) can be counted toward a minyan. If there are at least ten present, communal prayers can be said.

mitzvot: (Plural. Singular: *mitzvah*) The commandments or laws given by God. Traditionally Judaism holds there to be 613 such commandments, 248 positive ("thou shalt") and 365 negative ("thou shalt not"). A *mitzvah* is also understood to be a general good deed or act of kindness.

Mourner's Kaddish: A prayer praising God's holiness that is said by mourners at the gravesite and during prayer services for eleven months following the passing of a first-degree relative. Thereafter it is recited annually on the anniversary of that person's death. The prayer is in Aramaic.

parsha: The weekly portion of the Torah read aloud in synagogues around the world during public prayer. These portions are read in order through the year, beginning with Genesis and ending with Deuteronomy.

Pesach: (English: Passover) The biblical pilgrimage festival of Pesach celebrates the Jewish people's exodus from Egypt. Leavened products are forbidden for consumption during this seven-day holiday, such that preparation for Pesach is marked by the careful removal of bread and other leavened products from the home. Jews engage in a carefully scripted ritual meal called a *seder* on the first night (or first two nights) of the holiday in which the nation's liberation from slavery is retold. See *seder*.

sabra: (Hebrew: *tzabar*) A term used for Jews born in Israel. The label comes from the prickly-pear fruit of the same name, as sabras are said to be similarly tough and prickly on the outside but sweet on the inside.

seder: The special ritual meal held on the first night (first two nights outside the land of Israel) of the Passover holiday. The name comes from the word for "order" or "arrangement" as the meal follows a very specific ritual focused on the retelling of the exodus from Egypt. The meal is very lively and participatory, so that each person can come to feel as if he personally were redeemed from Egypt.

Shabbat: (Yiddish: *shabbes*; English: *sabbath*) The weekly seventh day of rest, emulating God's rest on the seventh day of creation. Shabbat lasts about twenty-five hours, beginning with the lighting of candles at sunset on Friday and ending at nightfall on Saturday night. It is traditionally marked by refraining from specific forms of creative activity, as defined by rabbinic tradition, which today has come to include driving and using money. Many Jews attend synagogue prayers on this day and have large meals with family and friends.

Shaharit: The morning prayer service. On weekdays it is the first of three prayer services for the day. *Shaharit* and the other prayer services can be prayed as a group in a *minyan*, or alone.

Shavuot: (Literally "weeks," Greek: Pentecost) The biblical pilgrimage Festival of Weeks comes after counting seven weeks from Passover. It celebrates God's giving of the Torah to the Jewish people at Mount Sinai and is traditionally marked by the eating of dairy products, night-long Torah study, and reading the book of Ruth.

Shehecheyanu: (Literally, "who has given us life") A blessing said to thank God on special occasions including annual holidays, life-cycle events, eating a particular fruit for the first time in the year, and wearing new clothing of value.

Shema: The central Jewish prayer and statement of faith whose name derives from the first two words *Shema Yisrael* ("Hear O Israel"). It consists of three biblical sections, Deuteronomy 6:4-9, 11:13-21, and Numbers 15:37-41. The *Shema* is recited twice a day by observant Jews, as well as at bedtime.

shiva: (Literally, "seven") Refers to the seven-day mourning period when a first-degree relative dies. This period is traditionally spent at home, focused on one's loss, while visitors come to comfort the mourner. There are several customs during this period including sitting on low stools, wearing a piece of torn clothing, and covering mirrors.

Sukkot: The seven-day Feast of Tabernacles celebrated in the fall, it is one of the three biblical pilgrimage festivals. It is celebrated by the building and dwelling in temporary shelters (*sukkot*) and the ritual use of "the four kinds:" palm frond (*lulav*), citron (*etrog*), myrtle (*hadas*), and willow (*arava*).

tallit: (Pronounced *tallis* in Yiddish) A four-cornered prayer shawl worn by Jewish men (and some Jewish women), with fringes attached at its corners. See *tzitzit*.

Tanakh: The Hebrew Bible. An acronym made up of the words *Torah* (Five Books of Moses), *Nevi'im* (Prophets), and *K'tuvim* (Writings).

tefillin: (English: "phylacteries") Worn by adult Jewish men (and, less commonly, women) during weekday morning prayer services. They consist of two leather boxes that contain biblical verses written on parchment (specifically, Exodus 13:9, 16 and Deuteronomy 6:8, 11:18). The boxes are bound with straps, one worn on the forehead and one on the upper arm.

tzitzit: (Hebrew: pronounced *tseet-tseet*; Yiddish: *tzitzis*) Specially knotted ritual fringes, or tassels, worn by Jews from antiquity up to today. They are expressly commanded in Numbers 15:37-41 and Deuteronomy 22:12, and are either attached to the four corners of an everyday undergarment (called a *tallit katan*) or the four corners of a prayer shawl (called a *tallit,* or *tallit gadol*). The number of strings and knots adds up to 613, the number of commandments in the Torah. The idea is that in looking upon the tzitzit, one is reminded to obey God and follow the commandments (*mitzvot*).

Yom Kippur: The annual Day of Atonement, based on Numbers 29:7. On this day, Jews fast from eating and drinking and spend much of the day in synagogue, with intense confession of guilt and prayers for forgiveness. It is the only day of the year marked by five prayer services. This day is considered the most important day of the year and is observed by most Jews, no matter how secular.

Zionism: Modern political movement that emerged in the nineteenth century advocating for a Jewish state in the land of Israel. Historically there were several distinct Zionist visions with their own particular emphases for the Jewish state.

NOTES

Introduction: On Being Monstrous

[1]See Mark Kinzer, *Postmissionary Messianic Judaism* (Grand Rapids, MI: Brazos, 2005), 198.

1 The Parting of the Ways

[1]Both of these streams of Judaism are products of Judaism's encounter with modernity, and both represent less traditional forms of Jewish practice. Neither of my parents grew up in homes where traditions such as *kashrut* (Jewish dietary laws) or *Shabbat* were strictly observed, and these pillars of traditional Jewish practice were also not a part of my upbringing.

[2]Jennifer M. Rosner, *Healing the Schism: Karl Barth, Franz Rosenzweig, and the New Jewish-Christian Encounter* (Bellingham, WA: Lexham, 2021). The book was previously published by Fortress in 2016.

[3]See R. Kendall Soulen, *The God of Israel and Christian Theology* (Minneapolis: Fortress, 1996), especially part two.

[4]See James Parkes, *The Conflict of the Church and the Synagogue: A Study in the Origins of Antisemitism* (London: Macmillan, 1969), 394-400.

2 The Excluded Middle

[1]In general, "anti-Judaism" is an aversion to the Jewish religion, while "antisemitism" is an aversion to Jews as a racial or ethnic group. A Jew can sidestep the first by ceasing to practice Judaism, whereas nothing a Jew can do allows them to escape the latter.

[2]*The Essential Luther*, ed. and trans. Tryntje Helfferich (Indianapolis: Hackett, 2018), 284-303.

[3]See, for example, the work of Amy-Jill Levine, Mark Nanos, Paula Fredriksen, and Pamela Eisenbaum. We will explore Paul's thought in much more detail in chap. 12.

[4]Jeremy Cohen, *Living Letters of the Law: Ideas of the Jew in Medieval Christianity* (Berkley: University of California Press, 1999).

[5]Portions of this chapter originally appeared in Jennifer M. Rosner, "Messianic Jews and Jewish-Christian Dialogue," in *Introduction to Messianic Judaism: Its Ecclesial Context and Biblical Foundations*, ed. David Rudolph and Joel Willitts (Grand Rapids, MI: Zondervan, 2013), 145-55.

[6]David Novak, "What to Seek and What to Avoid in Jewish-Christian Dialogue," in *Christianity in Jewish Terms*, ed. Tikva Frymer-Kensky et al. (Boulder, CO: Westview, 2000), 5.

[7]Paul G. Hiebert, "Conversion, Culture and Cognitive Categories," *Gospel in Context* 1, no. 4 (1978): 28.

[8]See, for example, Daniel Boyarin, *Borderlines: The Partition of Judaeo-Christianity* (Philadelphia: University of Pennsylvania Press, 2006).

3 LOST IN TRANSLATION

[1]At the beginning of my journey into Messianic Judaism, the most significant books for me were Kendall Soulen's *The God of Israel and Christian Theology* (Minneapolis: Fortress, 1996) and Mark Kinzer's *Postmissionary Messianic Judaism* (Grand Rapids, MI: Brazos, 2005). These two books wonderfully frame the key issues of Messianic Jewish identity and the problem of Christian replacement theology throughout history. Several years earlier, I had also read Lauren Winner's memoir *Girl Meets God*, and I was very aware of both the similarities and the differences between her journey and my own.

[2]Exodus 13:9, 16; Deuteronomy 6:8, 11:18.

[3]Portions of this chapter were published previously in Jennifer Rosner, "'Be Clean': Jesus and the World of Ritual Impurity," *Christianity Today*, April 20, 2021. Available at www.christianitytoday.com/ct/2021/may-june/dishonorable -discharge-jesus-and-world-of-ritual-impurity.html?share=GZrnEtN%2broO %2bb3iAbpc45Ew6Q7exgbGi.

[4]Jesus' description of the Pharisees' actions in this verse suggests that Jesus also wore tefillin.

[5]Matthew Thiessen, *Jesus and the Forces of Death: The Gospels' Portrayal of Ritual Impurity Within First-Century Judaism* (Grand Rapids, MI: Baker Academic, 2020), 2.

[6]See Mark D. Nanos, *Reading Romans Within Judaism* (Eugene, OR: Cascade, 2018), 126-33.

[7]Nanos does, however, have full annotations for the book of Romans in the *Jewish Annotated New Testament*, 2nd ed. (New York: Oxford, 2017).

[8]Amy-Jill Levine, *The Misunderstood Jew: The Church and the Scandal of the Jewish Jesus* (New York: HarperOne, 2007), 19.

[9]For example, the Nazis created a propaganda poster with Luther's face against a swastika backdrop, with the caption "Hitler's struggle and Luther's teaching provide the best defense for the German people." For a more thorough treatment of Hitler's usage of Luther, see Christopher J. Probst, *Demonizing the Jews: Luther and the Protestant Church in Nazi Germany* (Bloomington: Indiana University Press, 2012) and https://sojo.net/articles/nazis-exploited-martin-luther -s-legacy-berlin-exhibit-highlights-how (accessed December 30, 2020). It is also noteworthy that *Kristallnacht* was carried out on Luther's birthday.

[10]Dallas Willard, *The Spirit of the Disciplines: Understanding How God Changes Lives* (New York: HarperOne, 1999), xi. Willard offers a list of spiritual disciplines (including solitude, fasting, study, celebration, and fellowship) in *Spirit of the Disciplines*, chap. 9. Another excellent resource on the spiritual disciplines is Richard Foster, *Celebration of Discipline: The Path to Spiritual Growth* (San Francisco: Harper, 2002).

[11]Andy Stanley, *Irresistible: Reclaiming the New That Jesus Unleashed for the World* (Grand Rapids, MI: Zondervan, 2018), 245, 146.

[12]Quoted in David Van Biema, "Re-Judaizing Jesus," *Time Magazine*, March 13, 2008.

4 JESUS AND RITUAL PURITY

[1]Portions of this chapter were published previously in Jennifer Rosner, "'Be Clean': Jesus and the World of Ritual Impurity," *Christianity Today*, April 20, 2021. Available at www.christianitytoday.com/ct/2021/may-june/dishonorable -discharge-jesus-and-world-of-ritual-impurity.html?share=GZrnEtN%2broO% 2bb3iAbpc45Ew6Q7exgbGi.

[2]A. J. Jacobs, *The Year of Living Biblically* (New York: Simon & Schuster, 2007), 48-52.

[3]Portions of this chapter were originally published in Jennifer M. Rosner, "Jewish Christian Eschatology," in *Heaven, Hell, and the Afterlife: Eternity in Judaism, Christianity, and Islam*, ed. J. Harold Ellens, vol. 1, *End Time and Afterlife in Judaism* (Santa Barbara, CA: Praeger, 2013), 127-46. Used by permission.

[4]Mark Kinzer, *Israel's Messiah and the People of God: A Vision for Messianic Jewish Covenant Fidelity* (Eugene, OR: Cascade, 2011), 96; Abraham Joshua Heschel, *The Sabbath* (New York: Farrar, Straus and Giroux, 1951), 8, 21. The biblical narrative concretizes this connection by patterning the building of the tabernacle/temple after the six days of creation, with the tabernacle/temple as the telos of Israel's work mirroring the Sabbath as the telos of God's work (see Jon Levenson, *Sinai and Zion: An Entry into the Jewish Bible* [New York: HarperOne, 1985], 142-45).

[5]*M. Tamid* 7:4; *Genesis Rabbah* 17:5.

[6]Kinzer, *Israel's Messiah*, 104.

[7]See chap. 6 for the full Havdalah liturgy.

5 "The Land I Will Show You"

[1]See www.birthrightisrael.com/about-us.

[2]Hayim Halevy Donin, *To Be a Jew: A Guide to Jewish Observance in Contemporary Life* (New York: Basic Books, 1972), 13.

[3]Jonathan Sacks, *The Koren Siddur* (Koren: Jerusalem, 2009), 218; Mark S. Kinzer, *Jerusalem Crucified, Jerusalem Risen: The Resurrected Messiah, The Jewish People, and the Land of Promise* (Eugene, OR: Cascade, 2018), 242.

[4]See Deuteronomy 8:10.

[5]Franz Rosenzweig, *The Star of Redemption*, trans. Barbara E. Galli (Madison: University of Wisconsin Press, 2005), 319.

[6]For an excellent assessment of and challenge to this inconsistency, see Nicholas Brown, *For the Nation: Jesus, the Restoration of Israel and Articulating a Christian Ethic of Territorial Governance* (Eugene, OR: Pickwick, 2016).

[7]The Boycott, Divestment, Sanctions movement (see www.bdsmovement.net).

[8]Gerald McDermott, ed., *The New Christian Zionism: Fresh Perspectives on Israel & the Land* (Downers Grove, IL: IVP Academic, 2016).

[9]Joel Willitts, "Zionism in the Gospel of Matthew," in *The New Christian Zionism*, ed. Gerald McDermott, 109. See also Joel Willitts, *Matthew's Messianic Shepherd-King: In Search of "The Lost Sheep of the House of Israel"* (Berlin: De Gruyter, 2008), esp. chap. 6.

[10]Willitts, "Zionism in the Gospel of Matthew," 110-11.

[11]Willitts, "Zionism in the Gospel of Matthew," 111.

[12]See Gerald R. McDermott, *Israel Matters: Why Christians Must Think Differently About the People and the Land* (Grand Rapids, MI: Brazos, 2017), 29-30.

[13]Kinzer, *Jerusalem Crucified*, 10.

[14]Zionism as a movement emerged in the late nineteenth century and, though diverse, centered upon the return of the Jewish people to their national homeland and, now, focuses on the development and protection of the state of Israel. As with Zionism, anti-Zionism exists in various forms, all of which oppose the political actions (and, in some cases, the very existence) of the state of Israel. According to scholar Robert S. Wistrich,

Anti-Zionism has become the most dangerous and effective form of anti-Semitism in our time, through its systematic delegitimization, defamation, and demonization of Israel. Although not *a priori* anti-Semitic, the calls to dismantle the Jewish state, whether they come from Muslims, the Left, or the radical Right, increasingly rely on an anti-Semitic stereotypization of classic themes, such as the manipulative "Jewish lobby," the Jewish/Zionist "world conspiracy," and Jewish/Israeli "warmongers" (Robert S. Wistrich, *Jewish Political Studies Review* 16:3-4 [Fall 2004]).

6 BODIES

[1] Portions of this chapter were published previously in Jennifer Rosner, "'Be Clean': Jesus and the World of Ritual Impurity," *Christianity Today*, April 20, 2021. Available at www.christianitytoday.com/ct/2021/may-june/dishonorable -discharge-jesus-and-world-of-ritual-impurity.html?share=GZrnEtN%2broO %2bb3iAbpc45Ew6Q7exgbGi.

[2] Daniel Boyarin, *Carnal Israel: Reading Sex in Talmudic Culture* (Berkley: University of California Press, 1993), 5.

[3] Many Christian thinkers are reconsidering the notion of a "detachable soul." See for example Joel Green, *Body, Soul, and Human Life: The Nature of Humanity in the Bible* (Grand Rapids, MI: Baker Academic, 2008) and Nancey Murphy, *Bodies and Souls, or Spirited Bodies?* (Cambridge, MA: Cambridge University Press, 2006).

[4] Dallas Willard, *The Spirit of the Disciplines: Understanding How God Changes Lives* (New York: HarperCollins, 1988), 31 (emphasis mine).

[5] For a wonderful treatment of the distinction between heaven and new creation, see N. T. Wright, *Surprised by Hope: Rethinking Heaven, the Resurrection, and the Mission of the Church* (New York: HarperOne, 2008).

[6] Pirkei Avot 2:16.

[7] Adapted from Loren Eiseley, *The Star Thrower* (Chicago: Mariner, 1979), 169-85.

7 SIN AND THE FALL

[1] See www.yachad-beyeshua.org/documents.

[2] My dissertation is now published as *Healing the Schism: Karl Barth, Franz Rosenzweig, and the New Jewish-Christian Encounter* (Bellingham, WA: Lexham, 2021). It was previously published by Fortress Press in 2016.

[3] During my time as a doctoral student, I wrote an article on Christian vs. Jewish conceptions of sin and redemption, focusing on the theological writings of Karl Barth and Franz Rosenzweig, who were central theological figures in my dissertation. The article can be accessed at https://tjjt.cjs.utoronto.ca/wp-content /uploads/2013/11/Jennifer-M.-Rosner-Inward-Outward-Upward-Downward -Repentance-and-Redemption-in-the-Thought-of-Karl-Barth-and-Franz -Rosenzweig-JJT-Vol.-2.pdf.

[4] John Calvin, *Institutes of the Christian Religion*, ed. John T. McNeill, trans. Ford Lewis Battles (Louisville, KY: Westminster John Knox, 1960), II:246. While the

Augustinian-Reformed position described here is indeed a (the?) dominant narrative in Western Christianity, it is important to note that there are also other well-trod Christian understandings of these concepts. For a helpful overview of the spectrum, see *Original Sin and the Fall: Five Views*, ed. J. B. Stump and Chad Meister (Downers Grove, IL: IVP Academic, 2020).

[5]Calvin, *Institutes*, II:248.

[6]See Genesis Rabbah 9:7. *Midrash* is an ancient (and ongoing) tradition of Jewish commentary on passages in the biblical text.

[7]See www.yachad-beyeshua.org/.

[8]Jean-Marie Lustiger, *Dare to Believe: Addresses, Sermons, Interviews, 1981-1984* (New York: Crossroads, 1986), 91.

[9]Notably, Wyschogrod disagrees with David Novak, whose thought we engaged in chapter 2, in that Wyschogrod affirms Lustiger's ability to be both Jewish and Christian.

[10]Michael Wyschogrod, *Abraham's Promise: Judaism and Jewish-Christian Relations*, ed. R. Kendall Soulen (Grand Rapids, MI: Eerdmans, 2004), 206.

[11]Wyschogrod, *Abraham's Promise*, 207-8.

[12]See Maria Rosa Menocal, *The Ornament of the World: How Muslims, Christians, and Jews Created a Culture of Tolerance in Medieval Spain* (New York: Back Bay Books, 2002).

8 SABBATH

[1]Abraham Joshua Heschel, *The Sabbath: Its Meaning for Modern Man* (New York: Farrar, Straus and Giroux, 1951), 6. Notably, in Heschel's words, "The duty to work for six days is just as much a part of God's covenant with man as the duty to abstain from work on the seventh day" (28).

[2]Heschel, *Sabbath*, 10.

[3]Heschel, *Sabbath*, 20.

[4]Heschel, *Sabbath*, 29.

[5]*M. Tamid* 7:4.

[6]Heschel, *Sabbath*, 18.

[7]Heschel, *Sabbath*, 16-17.

[8]For more on the shift from Saturday to Sunday, see *From Sabbath to Lord's Day: A Biblical, Historical and Theological Investigation*, ed. D. A. Carson (Eugene, OR: Wipf & Stock, 2000) and Samuele Bacchiocchi, *From Sabbath to Sunday: A Historical Investigation of the Rise of Sunday Observance in Early Christianity* (Rome: Pontifical Gregorian University Press, 2014).

[9]*Epistle of Barnabas*, 15:9.

[10]Peter Hocken makes this point powerfully in *Azusa, Rome, and Zion: Pentecostal Faith, Catholic Reform, and Jewish Roots* (Eugene, OR: Pickwick, 2016), especially chap. 10.

9 THE SPIRIT

[1]Portions of this chapter were published previously in Jennifer Rosner, "'Be Clean': Jesus and the World of Ritual Impurity," *Christianity Today*, April 20, 2021. Available at www.christianitytoday.com/ct/2021/may-june/dishonorable -discharge-jesus-and-world-of-ritual-impurity.html?share=GZrnEtN%2broO% 2bb3iAbpc45Ew6Q7exgbGi. I have since coauthored a book that presents contrasting views on what the coming of the Spirit means with regard to Torah observance for Jewish followers of Jesus. See Joshua M. Lessard and Jennifer M. Rosner, *At the Foot of the Mountain: Two Views on Torah and the Spirit* (Eugene, OR: Resource Publications, 2021).

[2]See Mark S. Kinzer, *Postmissionary Messianic Judaism: Redefining Christian Engagement with the Jewish People* (Grand Rapids, MI: Brazos, 2005), esp. chaps. 2–4.

[3]For a deeply thoughtful commentary on a uniquely Hebraic definition of freedom, see Jonathan Sacks, "The Omer and the Politics of Torah," in *The Jonathan Sacks Haggadah* (Jerusalem: Koren, 2013).

[4]Rabbi Hayim Halevy Donin, *To Be a Jew* (New York: Basic Books, 1972), 240 (emphasis added).

[5]Portions of this chapter were originally published in Jennifer M. Rosner, "Jewish Christian Eschatology," in *Heaven, Hell, and the Afterlife: Eternity in Judaism, Christianity, and Islam*, ed. J. Harold Ellens, vol. 1, *End Time and Afterlife in Judaism* (Santa Barbara, CA: Praeger, 2013), 127-46. Used by permission.

[6]As commanded in Leviticus 23:42-43, one of the central aspects of this holiday is to "live in temporary shelters for seven days," in order to remember the temporary shelters the Jewish people lived in following the exodus from Egypt. For many Jews, this generally entails eating meals in a *sukkah* which is built for the occasion; some Jews (including Yonah, camping lover that he is) sleep in the *sukkah* as well.

[7]Stan Telchin, *Betrayed! How Do You Feel When You Are Successful, 50 and Jewish, and Your 21-Year-Old Daughter Tells You She Believes in Jesus?* (Grand Rapids, MI: Chosen, 1982).

10 SACRED DAYS

[1]Franz Rosenzweig, *The Star of Redemption*, trans. Barbara E. Galli (Madison: University of Wisconsin Press, 2005), 345.

[2]Many thanks to Michael Stone for his collaboration on this chapter.

[3]Yonah's tallit is pictured on the cover of this book.

[4]Later, at the Council of Antioch in AD 341, it was decreed that any Christians who defied this ruling and celebrated Passover with the Jews were to be "excluded from Communion and be outcasts from the Church."

11 GOD'S EX-WIFE

[1]This is a portion of the prayer titled "Ana Bakoach," which is recited as part of the traditional Friday night Shabbat liturgy in Judaism.

[2]R. Kendall Soulen, *The God of Israel and Christian Theology* (Minneapolis: Fortress, 1996), ix.

[3]Soulen, *God of Israel,* 16.

[4]Soulen, *God of Israel,* 1-2.

[5]Soulen, *God of Israel,* 109.

[6]Soulen addresses this issue in his later works, most notably in his essay, "The Standard Canonical Narrative and the Problem of Supersessionism," in *Introduction to Messianic Judaism: Its Ecclesial Context and Biblical Foundations,* ed. David Rudolph and Joel Willitts (Grand Rapids, MI: Zondervan, 2013), 282-91.

[7]This is a slightly modified version of the Tree of Life translation. The passage is notoriously difficult to translate; for an explanation of the issues involved, see Mark Kinzer, *Searching Her Own Mystery: Nostra Aetate, the Jewish People, and the Identity of the Church* (Eugene, OR: Cascade, 2015), 74-77, and *Postmissionary Messianic Judaism: Redefining Christian Engagement with the Jewish People* (Grand Rapids, MI: Brazos, 2005), 165-71.

[8]Markus Barth, *Ephesians 1-3* (Garden City, NY: Doubleday, 1974), 337.

12 PAUL

[1]*Peyos* literally means "sides" or "edges" and refers to the sidelocks or sidecurls worn by many Orthodox Jewish men as a practical implementation of Leviticus 19:27, which reads, "Do not cut the hair at the sides of your head or clip off the edges of your beard."

[2]For an excellent (though not entirely up-to-date) overview of these developments in Pauline scholarship, see Magnus Zetterholm, *Approaches to Paul: A Student's Guide to Recent Scholarship* (Minneapolis: Fortress, 2009).

[3]This feature of Paul Within Judaism scholarship is especially significant for Mark Kinzer's notion of "bilateral ecclesiology."

[4]David Novak, "What to Seek and What to Avoid in Jewish-Christian Dialogue," in *Christianity in Jewish Terms,* ed. Tikva Frymer-Kensky et al. (Boulder, CO: Westview, 2000), 5.

13 A WAY FORWARD

[1]Chabad-Lubavitch is an Orthodox Jewish movement and organization that is especially focused on outreach to the Jewish people. Chabad sends emissaries to the four corners of the globe with the goal of reaching out to Jews and drawing them closer to Judaism.

[2]See, for example, the Willowbank Declaration of the World Evangelical Fellowship (issued in 1989) and the Berlin Declaration of the World Evangelical Alliance (issued in 2008).

[3]The word *intifada* means "uprising" in Arabic and is used to describe historic groundswells of tension between the Palestinians and the state of Israel. The First Intifada took place in the late 1980s and ended with the signing of the Oslo Accords in 1993. The Second Intifada began in September 2000 in response to Ariel Sharon's provocative visit to the Temple Mount. Many began referring to the period described here, which began in July 2014, as the Third Intifada.

[4]Jennifer M. Rosner, *Healing the Schism: Karl Barth, Franz Rosenzweig and the New Jewish-Christian Encounter* (Bellingham, WA: Lexham, 2021), 3.

[5]Rosner, *Healing the Schism*, 247-48.

[6]Franz Rosenzweig, *The Star of Redemption*, trans. Barbara E. Galli (Madison: University of Wisconsin Press, 2005), 418.

EPILOGUE: THE JEWISH GOSPEL

[1]See David Rudolph, "Guidelines for Healthy Theological Discussion," in *The Borough Park Papers. Symposium I: The Gospel and the Jewish People* (Clarksville, MD: Messianic Jewish Publishers, 2012), 7-14; William Isaacs, *Dialogue: The Art of Thinking Together* (New York: Currency, 1999), 98-99.

[2]This assignment, which is one of my favorites, was inspired by Kendall Soulen's one-sentence gospel in *The God of Israel and Christian Theology* (Minneapolis: Fortress, 1996), 157.

[3]I'm thankful to my friend Fr. David Neuhaus for making this point clear to me in a deeper way.

ABOUT THE AUTHOR

Jennifer Rosner is affiliate assistant professor of systematic theology at Fuller Theological Seminary. She also holds academic posts at Azusa Pacific University, The King's University, and Messianic Jewish Theological Institute.

She is the author of *Healing the Schism: Karl Barth, Franz Rosenzweig and the New Jewish-Encounter,* and coauthor of *At the Foot of the Mountain: Two Views on Torah and the Spirit.* She also edited Mark Kinzer's collection of essays titled *Israel's Messiah and the People of God: A Vision for Messianic Jewish Covenant Fidelity.*

You can find her online (and subscribe to her monthly newsletter) at

www.jenrosner.com

Twitter: @JenRosner

Facebook: JenMRosner